SINGLE-PARENT FAMILIES

Other Books in the At Issue Series:

Affirmative Action
Business Ethics
Domestic Violence
Environmental Justice
Ethnic Conflict
Immigration Policy
The Jury System
Legalizing Drugs
The Media and Politics
The Militia Movement
Policing the Police
Rape on Campus
Smoking
The Spread of AIDS
The United Nations
U.S. Policy Toward China
Voting Behavior
Welfare Reform
What Is Sexual Harassment?

SINGLE-PARENT FAMILIES

David Bender, *Publisher*

Bruno Leone, *Executive Editor*

Scott Barbour, *Managing Editor*

Brenda Stalcup, *Series Editor*

Karin L. Swisher, *Book Editor*

7/97

An Opposing Viewpoints ® Series

Greenhaven Press, Inc.

San Diego, California

Library of Congress Cataloging-in-Publication Data

Single-parent families / Karin L. Swisher, book editor.
        p.   cm. — (At issue)
    Includes bibliographical references (p.   ) and index.
    ISBN 1-56510-544-3 (Lib. : alk. paper) —   ᶜ⁾
ISBN 1-56510-543-5 (Pbk. : alk. paper.)
    1. Single-parent family—United States. 2. Single mothers—
United
    States. I. Swisher, Karin L., 1966– . II. Series: At issue (San Diego,
Calif.).
    HQ759.915.S5   1997
    306.85'6—dc20   96-33555
                                                                            CIP

©1997 by Greenhaven Press, Inc., PO Box 289009,
San Diego, CA 92198-9009

Printed in the U.S.A.

Table of Contents

	Page
Introduction	7
1. Single-Parent Families Are Harmful *Barbara Dafoe Whitehead*	10
2. Divorce Harms Children *Karl Zinsmeister*	41
3. Single-Parent Families Contribute to Violent Crime *Wade C. Mackey*	49
4. Single-Parent Families Contribute to the Breakdown of Society *Jean Bethke Elshtain*	53
5. Fathers Are Important to Families *David Blankenhorn*	60
6. The Harmful Effects of Single-Parent Families Are Exaggerated *Arlene Skolnick and Stacey Rosencranz*	62
7. Single-Parent Families Have Been Unfairly Stigmatized *Iris Marion Young*	71
8. The Harm Caused by Unwed Mothers Is Exaggerated *Clarence Page*	79
9. Single Mothers Are Unfairly Blamed for Poverty *Holly Sklar*	82
10. Single Motherhood Is a Legitimate Choice *Katha Pollitt*	98
Organizations to Contact	101
Bibliography	104
Index	107

Introduction

In May 1992, Vice President Dan Quayle suggested that a breakdown of the nuclear family was among the causes of recent riots in Los Angeles in which over fifty people had died. "I believe the lawless social anarchy which we saw is directly related to the breakdown of family structure, personal responsibility and social order in too many areas of our society," Quayle remarked. He went on to criticize society's increasingly permissive attitude toward out-of-wedlock childbearing, pointing specifically to the treatment of the issue in the television sitcom *Murphy Brown*. "It doesn't help matters when prime time TV has Murphy Brown—a character who supposedly epitomizes today's intelligent, highly paid, professional woman—mocking the importance of fathers by bearing a child alone and calling it just another 'lifestyle choice.'"

Quayle's speech, especially his reference to Murphy Brown, provoked an outpouring of commentary. Numerous Americans agreed with Quayle, expressing concern that the "traditional family" and "family values" were being undermined by a public morality that too readily condoned unwed motherhood and divorce. Many also agreed with Quayle's argument that the media and popular culture were to blame for promoting loose sexual values and immoral lifestyles.

Others took exception to Quayle's statements. Some, seeing his speech as a moralistic attack on single mothers, responded by insisting that most single mothers work hard to provide for their children and to raise them well. Others considered Quayle's view of the traditional family as nostalgic and unrealistic, out of touch with the social and economic realities of life in contemporary America. The character Murphy Brown, played by actress Candice Bergen, directly responded to Quayle in a subsequent episode of the show. In words that doubtlessly resonated with many Americans, she declared, "Perhaps it's time for the vice president to expand his definition [of family] and recognize that whether by choice or circumstance families come in all shapes and sizes. And ultimately, what really defines a family is commitment, caring and love."

The intensity of the public reaction to Quayle's speech suggests that his comments touched on an issue of concern to a large number of people. Indeed, many commentators have expressed alarm about the increase in single-parent families over the past four decades. In 1960, they point out, 5.8 million American children lived in single-parent families; by 1996 that number had risen to 18 million. This growth has been fueled by an increasing rate of out-of-wedlock childbearing. In 1960, 5.3 percent of American babies were born to unwed mothers; that rate has increased to 30 percent. These numbers are even higher for African Americans: As of 1992, 68 percent of African American babies were born to unmarried women. A rising divorce rate has also contributed to the growing number of single-parent families. The U.S. divorce rate rose nearly 250 percent between 1960 and 1980; it then leveled off at what is now the highest rate in the industrialized world. It is commonly noted that about half of the marriages undertaken today will end in divorce.

Much of the debate over single-parent families focuses on how these trends affect children. Many social scientists contend that children raised in single-parent homes are more likely to experience a variety of problems than are children raised in two-parent homes. According to Lloyd Eby, assistant editor of the *World & I* magazine, and Charles A. Donovan, a senior policy consultant at the Family Research Council, "The sociological evidence now available shows conclusively that children suffer when they grow up in any family situation other than an intact two-parent family formed by their biological father and mother who are married to each other." Some sociological studies suggest that children of single parents are more likely to be poor, to commit crimes, to use drugs, to do poorly in school, or to become pregnant.

Commentators insist that these problems affect not only the children involved but also the larger society, which must pay the costs for increased crime, disease, poverty, and other forms of societal breakdown. Many conservatives insist that because most single-parent families are headed by women, society is particularly threatened by the presence of large numbers of adolescent males who have been raised without the guidance and discipline that is typically provided by a father. According to David Blankenhorn, the founder and president of the Institute for American Values and the author of *Fatherless America: Confronting Our Most Urgent Social Problem*, "Fatherlessness is the most harmful demographic trend of this generation. It is the leading cause of declining child well-being in our society. It is also the engine driving our most urgent social problems, from crime to adolescent pregnancy to child sexual abuse to domestic violence against women."

While most people agree that children are better off in families with two parents (as long as both parents are nonabusive), many believe that the adverse impact of single-parent families on children has been exaggerated. According to Sara S. McLanahan, a professor of sociology and public affairs at Princeton University, children who grow up with one parent are "disadvantaged across a broad array of outcomes"; they are more likely to drop out of school, commit crime, or become pregnant. However, she concludes, "the evidence . . . does not show that family disruption is the principal cause" of these problems. According to McLanahan, "If all children lived in two-parent families, teen motherhood and idleness would be less common, but the bulk of these problems would remain."

In addition, some social scientists and others argue that the causal connection between single-parent families and social problems is unclear. While most experts concede that children from single-parent families are more likely to experience problems such as poor school performance and poverty, many believe it is erroneous to automatically assume that these difficulties are caused by the absence of one parent. According to Arlene Skolnick, a research psychologist at the University of California at Berkeley, and Stacey Rosencranz, a graduate student at Stanford University,

"Single parenthood may be correlated with many problems affecting children, but the causes may lie elsewhere—for example, in economic and emotional problems affecting parents that lead to difficulties raising children and greater chances of divorce." Other commentators contend that for the large number of single-parent families who live in inner cities, a shortage of educational and employment opportunities is more likely to impact the quality of children's lives than the number of parents they have.

Whether children are more likely to suffer social and economic problems when raised by one parent rather than two is a central theme explored in *At Issue: Single-Parent Families*. Throughout this anthology, Quayle's concerns about "the breakdown of the family structure" are echoed and disputed as authors debate the implications of the growing number of single-parent families.

1

Single-Parent Families Are Harmful

Barbara Dafoe Whitehead

Barbara Dafoe Whitehead is a social historian in Amherst, Massachusetts.

Divorce and out-of-wedlock childbearing are now epidemic in American society. Both forms of disrupted families are harmful to children and to society. The children of single parents are more likely to do poorly in school, commit crimes, and become single parents themselves. In addition, the increase in single-parent families contributes to such social problems as poverty, crime, and a decline in the quality of public education.

Divorce and out-of-wedlock childbirth are transforming the lives of American children. In the postwar generation more than 80 percent of children grew up in a family with two biological parents who were married to each other. By 1980 only 50 percent could expect to spend their entire childhood in an intact family. If current trends continue, less than half of all children born today will live continuously with their own mother and father throughout childhood. Most American children will spend several years in a single-mother family. Some will eventually live in stepparent families, but because stepfamilies are more likely to break up than intact (by which I mean two-biological-parent) families, an increasing number of children will experience family breakup two or even three times during childhood.

The effects of single-parent families

According to a growing body of social-scientific evidence, children in families disrupted by divorce and out-of-wedlock birth do worse than children in intact families on several measures of well-being. Children in single-parent families are six times as likely to be poor. They are also likely to stay poor longer. Twenty-two percent of children in one-parent families will experience poverty during childhood for seven years or more, as

Barbara Dafoe Whitehead, "Dan Quayle Was Right," *Atlantic Monthly*, April 1993. Reprinted by permission of the author.

compared with only two percent of children in two-parent families. A 1988 survey by the National Center for Health Statistics found that children in single-parent families are two to three times as likely as children in two-parent families to have emotional and behavioral problems. They are also more likely to drop out of high school, to get pregnant as teenagers, to abuse drugs, and to be in trouble with the law. Compared with children in intact families, children from disrupted families are at a much higher risk for physical or sexual abuse.

Contrary to popular belief, many children do not "bounce back" after divorce or remarriage. Difficulties that are associated with family breakup often persist into adulthood. Children who grow up in single-parent or stepparent families are less successful as adults, particularly in the two domains of life—love and work—that are most essential to happiness. Needless to say, not all children experience such negative effects. However, research shows that many children from disrupted families have a harder time achieving intimacy in a relationship, forming a stable marriage, or even holding a steady job.

> *If current trends continue, less than half of all children born today will live continuously with their own mother and father throughout childhood.*

Despite this growing body of evidence, it is nearly impossible to discuss changes in family structure without provoking angry protest. Many people see the discussion as no more than an attack on struggling single mothers and their children: Why blame single mothers when they are doing the very best they can? After all, the decision to end a marriage or a relationship is wrenching, and few parents are indifferent to the painful burden this decision imposes on their children. Many take the perilous step toward single parenthood as a last resort, after their best efforts to hold a marriage together have failed. Consequently, it can seem particularly cruel and unfeeling to remind parents of the hardships their children might suffer as a result of family breakup. Other people believe that the dramatic changes in family structure, though regrettable, are impossible to reverse. Family breakup is an inevitable feature of American life, and anyone who thinks otherwise is indulging in nostalgia or trying to turn back the clock. Since these new family forms are here to stay, the reasoning goes, we must accord respect to single parents, not criticize them. Typical is the view expressed by a Brooklyn woman in a recent letter to the *New York Times*: "Let's stop moralizing or blaming single parents and unwed mothers, and give them the respect they have earned and the support they deserve."

Such views are not to be dismissed. Indeed, they help to explain why family structure is such an explosive issue for Americans. The debate about it is not simply about the social-scientific evidence, although that is surely an important part of the discussion. It is also a debate over deeply held and often conflicting values. How do we begin to reconcile our long-standing belief in equality and diversity with an impressive body of evidence that suggests that not all family structures produce equal outcomes for children? How can we square traditional notions of public support for dependent women and children with a belief in women's right to pursue autonomy and independence in childbearing and child-rearing? How do we uphold the freedom of adults to pursue individual happiness in their private relationships and at the same time respond to the needs of children for stability, security, and permanence in their family lives? What do we do when the interests of adults and children conflict? These are the difficult issues at stake in the debate over family structure.

Past discussions on families

In the past these issues have turned out to be too difficult and too politically risky for debate. In the mid-1960s Daniel Patrick Moynihan, then an assistant secretary of labor, was denounced as a racist for calling attention to the relationship between the prevalence of black single-mother families and the lower socioeconomic standing of black children. For nearly twenty years the policy and research communities backed away from the entire issue. In 1980 the Carter Administration convened a historic White House Conference on Families, designed to address the growing problems of children and families in America. The result was a prolonged, publicly subsidized quarrel over the definition of "family." No President since has tried to hold a national family conference. In 1992, at a time when the rate of out-of-wedlock births had reached a historic high, Vice President Dan Quayle was ridiculed for criticizing Murphy Brown. In short, every time the issue of family structure has been raised, the response has been first controversy, then retreat, and finally silence.

Yet it is also risky to ignore the issue of changing family structure. In recent years the problems associated with family disruption have grown. Overall child well-being has declined, despite a decrease in the number of children per family, an increase in the educational level of parents, and historically high levels of public spending. After dropping in the 1960s and 1970s, the proportion of children in poverty has increased dramatically, from 15 percent in 1970 to 20 percent in 1990, while the percentage of adult Americans in poverty has remained roughly constant. The teen suicide rate has more than tripled. Juvenile crime has increased and become more violent. School performance has continued to decline. There are no signs that these trends are about to reverse themselves.

If we fail to come to terms with the relationship between family structure and declining child well-being, then it will be increasingly difficult to improve children's life prospects, no matter how many new programs the federal government funds. Nor will we be able to make progress in bettering school performance or reducing crime or improving the quality of the nation's future work force—all domestic problems closely connected to family breakup. Worse, we may contribute to the problem by pursuing policies that actually increase family instability and breakup.

From death to divorce

Across time and across cultures, family disruption has been regarded as an event that threatens a child's well-being and even survival. This view is rooted in a fundamental biological fact: unlike the young of almost any other species, the human child is born in an abjectly helpless and immature state. Years of nurture and protection are needed before the child can achieve physical independence. Similarly, it takes years of interaction with at least one but ideally two or more adults for a child to develop into a socially competent adult. Children raised in virtual isolation from human beings, though physically intact, display few recognizably human behaviors. The social arrangement that has proved most successful in ensuring the physical survival and promoting the social development of the child is the family unit of the biological mother and father. Consequently, any event that permanently denies a child the presence and protection of a parent jeopardizes the life of the child.

The classic form of family disruption is the death of a parent. Throughout history this has been one of the risks of childhood. Mothers frequently died in childbirth, and it was not unusual for both parents to die before the child was grown. As recently as the early decades of the 20th century children commonly suffered the death of at least one parent. Almost a quarter of the children born in this country in 1900 lost one parent by the time they were fifteen years old. Many of these children lived with their widowed parent, often in a household with other close relatives. Others grew up in orphanages and foster homes.

Contrary to popular belief, many children do not "bounce back" after divorce or remarriage.

The meaning of parental death, as it has been transmitted over time and faithfully recorded in world literature and lore, is unambiguous and essentially unchanging. It is universally regarded as an untimely and tragic event. Death permanently severs the parent-child bond, disrupting forever one of the child's earliest and deepest human attachments. It also deprives a child of the presence and protection of an adult who has a biological stake in, as well as an emotional commitment to, the child's survival and well-being. In short, the death of a parent is the most extreme and severe loss a child can suffer.

Because a child is so vulnerable in a parent's absence, there has been a common cultural response to the death of a parent: an outpouring of support from family, friends, and strangers alike. The surviving parent and child are united in their grief as well as their loss. Relatives and friends share in the loss and provide valuable emotional and financial assistance to the bereaved family. Other members of the community show sympathy for the child, and public assistance is available for those who need it. This cultural understanding of parental death has formed the basis for a tradition of public support to widows and their children. Indeed, as recently as the beginning of this century widows were the only mothers eligible for pensions in many states, and today widows with children receive more-generous welfare benefits from Survivors Insurance than do other single mothers with children who depend on Aid to Families With Dependent Children.

It has taken thousands upon thousands of years to reduce the threat of parental death. Not until the middle of the twentieth century did parental death cease to be a commonplace event for children in the

United States. By then advances in medicine had dramatically reduced mortality rates for men and women.

Social sanctions

At the same time, other forms of family disruption—separation, divorce, out-of-wedlock birth—were held in check by powerful religious, social, and legal sanctions. Divorce was widely regarded both as a deviant behavior, especially threatening to mothers and children, and as a personal lapse: "Divorce is the public acknowledgment of failure," a 1940s sociology textbook noted. Out-of-wedlock birth was stigmatized, and stigmatization is a powerful means of regulating behavior, as any smoker or overeater will testify. Sanctions against nonmarital childbirth discouraged behavior that hurt children and exacted compensatory behavior that helped them. Shotgun marriages and adoption, two common responses to nonmarital birth, carried a strong message about the risks of premarital sex and created an intact family for the child.

Consequently, children did not have to worry much about losing a parent through divorce or never having had one because of nonmarital birth. After a surge in divorces following the Second World War, the rate leveled off. Only 11 percent of children born in the 1950s would by the time they turned eighteen see their parents separate or divorce. Out-of-wedlock childbirth barely figured as a cause of family disruption. In the 1950s and early 1960s, five percent of the nation's births were out of wedlock. Blacks were more likely than whites to bear children outside marriage, but the majority of black children born in the twenty years after the Second World War were born to married couples. The rate of family disruption reached a historic low point during those years.

A new standard of family security and stability was established in postwar America. For the first time in history the vast majority of the nation's children could expect to live with married biological parents throughout childhood. Children might still suffer other forms of adversity—poverty, racial discrimination, lack of educational opportunity—but only a few would be deprived of the nurture and protection of a mother and a father. No longer did children have to be haunted by the classic fears vividly dramatized in folklore and fable—that their parents would die, that they would have to live with a stepparent and stepsiblings, or that they would be abandoned. These were the years when the nation confidently boarded up orphanages and closed foundling hospitals, certain that such institutions would never again be needed. In movie theaters across the country parents and children could watch the drama of parental separation and death, in the great Disney classics, secure in the knowledge that such nightmare visions as the death of Bambi's mother and the wrenching separation of Dumbo from his mother were only make-believe.

In the 1960s the rate of family disruption suddenly began to rise. After inching up over the course of a century, the divorce rate soared. Throughout the 1950s and early 1960s the divorce rate held steady at fewer than ten divorces a year per 1,000 married couples. Then, beginning in about 1965, the rate increased sharply, peaking at twenty-three divorces per 1,000 marriages by 1979. (In 1974 divorce passed death as the leading cause of family breakup.) The rate has leveled off at about twenty-one divorces per 1,000 marriages—the figure for 1991. The out-of-wedlock birth rate also jumped. It went from five percent in 1960 to 27 percent in 1990. In 1990 close to 57 percent of births among black mothers were nonmarital, and about 17 percent among white mothers. Altogether, about one out of every four women who had a child in 1990 was not married. With rates of divorce and nonmarital birth so high, family disruption is at its peak. Never before have so many children experienced family breakup caused by events other than death. Each year a million children go through divorce or separation and almost as many more are born out of wedlock.

Half of all marriages now end in divorce. Following divorce, many people enter new relationships. Some begin living together. Nearly half of all cohabiting couples have children in the household. Fifteen percent have new children together. Many cohabiting couples eventually get married. However, both cohabiting and remarried couples are more likely to break up than couples in first marriages. Even social scientists find it hard to keep pace with the complexity and velocity of such patterns. In the revised edition of his book *Marriage, Divorce, Remarriage*, the sociologist Andrew Cherlin ruefully comments: "If there were a truth-in-labeling law for books, the title of this edition should be something long and unwieldy like *Cohabitation, Marriage, Divorce, More Cohabitation, and Probably Remarriage.*"

It is . . . risky to ignore the issue of changing family structure.

Under such conditions growing up can be a turbulent experience. In many single-parent families children must come to terms with the parent's love life and romantic partners. Some children live with cohabiting couples, either their own unmarried parents or a biological parent and a live-in partner. Some children born to cohabiting parents see their parents break up. Others see their parents marry, but 56 percent of them (as compared with 31 percent of the children born to married parents) later see their parents' marriages fall apart. All told, about three quarters of children born to cohabiting couples will live in a single-parent home at least briefly. One of every four children growing up in the 1990s will eventually enter a stepfamily. According to one survey, nearly half of all children in stepparent families will see their parents divorce again by the time they reach their late teens. Since 80 percent of divorced fathers remarry, things get even more complicated when the romantic or marital history of the noncustodial parent, usually the father, is taken into account. Consequently, as it affects a significant number of children, family disruption is best understood not as a single event but as a string of disruptive events: separation, divorce, life in a single-parent family, life with a parent and live-in lover, the remarriage of one or both parents, life in one stepparent family combined with visits to another stepparent family; the breakup of one or both stepparent families. And so on. This is one reason why public schools have a hard time knowing whom to call in an emergency.

Given its dramatic impact on children's lives, one might reasonably expect that this historic level of family disruption would be viewed with alarm, even regarded as a national crisis. Yet this has not been the case. In recent years some people have argued that these trends pose a serious threat to children and to the nation as a whole, but they are dismissed as declinists, pessimists, or nostalgists, unwilling or unable to accept the new facts of life. The dominant view is that the changes in family structure are, on balance, positive.

A shift in the social metric

There are several reasons why this is so, but the fundamental reason is that at some point in the 1970s Americans changed their minds about the meaning of these disruptive behaviors. What had once been regarded as hostile to children's best interests was now considered essential to adults' happiness. In the 1950s most Americans believed that parents should stay in an unhappy marriage for the sake of the children. The assumption was that a divorce would damage the children, and the prospect of such damage gave divorce its meaning. By the mid-1970s a majority of Americans rejected that view. Popular advice literature reflected the shift. A book on divorce published in the mid-1940s tersely asserted: "Children are entitled to the affection and *association* of two parents, not one." Thirty years later another popular divorce book proclaimed just the opposite: "A two-parent home is not the only emotional structure within which a child can be happy and healthy. . . . The parents who take care of themselves will be best able to take care of their children." At about the same time, the long-standing taboo against out-of-wedlock childbirth also collapsed. By the mid-1970s three-fourths of Americans said that it was not morally wrong for a woman to have a child outside marriage.

Once the social metric shifts from child well-being to adult well-being, it is hard to see divorce and nonmarital birth in anything but a positive light. However distressing and difficult they may be, both of these behaviors can hold out the promise of greater adult choice, freedom, and happiness. For unhappy spouses, divorce offers a way to escape a troubled or even abusive relationship and make a fresh start. For single parents, remarriage is a second try at marital happiness as well as a chance for relief from the stress, loneliness, and economic hardship of raising a child alone. For some unmarried women, nonmarital birth is a way to beat the biological clock, avoid marrying the wrong man, and experience the pleasures of motherhood. Moreover, divorce and out-of-wedlock birth involve a measure of agency and choice; they are man- and woman-made events. To be sure, not everyone exercises choice in divorce or nonmarital birth. Men leave wives for younger women, teenage girls get pregnant accidentally—yet even these unhappy events reflect the expansion of the boundaries of freedom and choice.

This cultural shift helps explain what otherwise would be inexplicable: the failure to see the rise in family disruption as a severe and troubling national problem. It explains why there is virtually no widespread public sentiment for restigmatizing either of these classically disruptive behaviors and no sense—no public consensus—that they can or should be avoided in the future. On the contrary, the prevailing opinion is that we should accept the changes in family structure as inevitable and devise new forms of public and private support for single-parent families.

The view from Hollywood

With its affirmation of the liberating effects of divorce and nonmarital childbirth, this opinion is a fixture of American popular culture today. Madison Avenue and Hollywood did not invent these behaviors, as their highly paid publicists are quick to point out, but they have played an influential role in defending and even celebrating divorce and unwed motherhood. More precisely, they have taken the raw material of demography and fashioned it into a powerful fantasy of individual renewal and rebirth. Consider, for example, the teaser for *People* magazine's cover story on Joan Lunden's divorce: "After the painful end of her 13-year marriage, the *Good Morning America* cohost is discovering a new life as a single mother—and as her own woman." *People* does not dwell on the anguish Lunden and her children might have experienced over the breakup of their family, or the difficulties of single motherhood, even for celebrity mothers. Instead, it celebrates Joan Lunden's steps toward independence and a better life. *People*, characteristically, focuses on her shopping: in the first weeks after her breakup Lunden leased "a brand-new six-bedroom, 8,000 square foot" house and then went to Bloomingdale's, where she scooped up sheets, pillows, a toaster, dishes, seven televisions, and roomfuls of fun furniture that was "totally unlike the serious traditional pieces she was giving up."

This is not just the view taken in supermarket magazines. Even the conservative bastion of the greeting-card industry, Hallmark, offers a line of cards commemorating divorce as liberation. "Think of your former marriage as a record album," says one Contemporary card. "It was full of music—both happy and sad. But what's important now is . . . YOU! the recently released HOT, NEW, SINGLE! You're going to be at the TOP OF THE CHARTS!" Another card reads: "Getting divorced can be very healthy! Watch how it improves your circulation! Best of luck! . . ." Hallmark's hip Shoebox Greetings division depicts two female praying mantises. Mantis One: "It's tough being a single parent." Mantis Two: "Yeah . . . Maybe we shouldn't have eaten our husbands."

Divorce is a tired convention in Hollywood, but unwed parenthood is very much in fashion: in one year, babies were born to Warren Beatty and Annette Bening, Jack Nicholson and Rebecca Broussard, and Eddie Murphy and Nicole Mitchell. *Vanity Fair* celebrated Jack Nicholson's fatherhood with a cover story in April 1992 called "Happy Jack." What made Jack happy, it turned out, was no-fault fatherhood. He and Broussard, the twenty-nine-year-old mother of his children, lived in separate houses. Nicholson said, "It's an unusual arrangement, but the last twenty-five years or so have shown me that I'm not good at cohabitation. . . . I see Rebecca as much as any other person who is cohabiting. And *she* prefers it. I think most people would in a more honest and truthful world." As for more-permanent commitments, the man who is not good at cohabitation said: "I don't discuss marriage much with Rebecca. Those discussions are the very thing I'm trying to avoid. I'm after this immediate real thing. That's all I believe in." (Perhaps Nicholson should have had the discussion. Not long after the story appeared, Broussard broke off the relationship.)

As this story shows, unwed parenthood is thought of not only as a way to find happiness but also as a way to exhibit such virtues as honesty and courage. A similar argument was offered in defense of Murphy Brown's unwed motherhood. Many of Murphy's fans were quick to point out that Murphy suffered over her decision to bear a child out of wedlock. Faced with an accidental pregnancy and a faithless lover, she agonized over her plight and, after much mental anguish, bravely decided to go ahead. In short, having a baby without a husband represented a higher level of maternal devotion and sacrifice than having a baby with a husband. Murphy was not just exercising her rights as a woman; she was exhibiting true moral heroism.

On the night Murphy Brown became an unwed mother, 34 million Americans tuned in, and CBS posted a 35 percent share of the audience. The show did not stir significant protest at the grass roots and lost none of its advertisers. The actress Candice Bergen subsequently appeared on the cover of nearly every women's and news magazine in the country and received an honorary degree at the University of Pennsylvania as well as an Emmy award. The show's creator, Diane English, popped up in Hanes stocking ads. Judged by conventional measures of approval, Murphy Brown's motherhood was a hit at the box office.

Discrediting families

Increasingly, the media depicts the married two-parent family as a source of pathology. According to a spate of celebrity memoirs and interviews, the married-parent family harbors terrible secrets of abuse, violence, and incest. A bumper sticker I saw in Amherst, Massachusetts, read UNSPOKEN TRADITIONAL FAMILY VALUES: ABUSE, ALCOHOLISM, INCEST. The pop therapist John Bradshaw explains away this generation's problems with the dictum that 96 percent of families are dysfunctional, made that way by the addicted society we live in. David Lynch creates a new aesthetic of creepiness by juxtaposing scenes of traditional family life with images of seduction and perversion. A Boston-area museum puts on an exhibit called "Goodbye to Apple Pie," featuring several artists' visions of child abuse, including one mixed-media piece with knives poking through a little girl's skirt. The piece is titled *Father Knows Best*.

No one would claim that two-parent families are free from conflict, violence, or abuse. However, the attempt to discredit the two-parent family can be understood as part of what Daniel Patrick Moynihan has described as a larger effort to accommodate higher levels of social deviance. "The amount of deviant behavior in American society has increased beyond the levels the community can 'afford to recognize,'" Moynihan argues. One response has been to normalize what was once considered deviant behavior, such as out-of-wedlock birth. An accompanying response has been to detect deviance in what once stood as a social norm, such as the married-couple family. Together these responses reduce the acknowledged levels of deviance by eroding earlier distinctions between the normal and the deviant.

Several recent studies describe family life in its postwar heyday as the seedbed of alcoholism and abuse. According to Stephanie Coontz, the author of the book *The Way We Never Were: American Families and the Nostalgia Trap*, family life for married mothers in the 1950s consisted of "booze, bowling, bridge, and boredom." Coontz writes: "Few would have guessed that radiant Marilyn Van Derbur, crowned Miss America in 1958, had been sexually violated by her wealthy, respectable father from the time she was five until she was eighteen, when she moved away to college." Even the budget-stretching casserole comes under attack as a sign of culinary dysfunction. According to one food writer, this homely staple of postwar family life brings back images of "the good mother of the 50's . . . locked in Ozzie and Harriet land, unable to move past the canvas of a Corning Ware dish, the palette of a can of Campbell's soup, the mushy dominion of which she was queen."

Nevertheless, the popular portrait of family life does not simply reflect the views of a cultural elite, as some have argued. There is strong support at the grass roots for much of this view of family change. Survey after survey shows that Americans are less inclined than they were a generation ago to value sexual fidelity, lifelong marriage, and parenthood as worthwhile personal goals. Motherhood no longer defines adult womanhood, as everyone knows; equally important is the fact that fatherhood has declined as a norm for men. In 1976 less than half as many fathers as in 1957 said that providing for children was a life goal. The proportion of working men who found marriage and children burdensome and restrictive more than doubled in the same period. Fewer than half of all adult Americans today regard the idea of sacrifice for others as a positive moral virtue.

Dinosaurs divorce

It is true that many adults benefit from divorce or remarriage. According to one study, nearly 80 percent of divorced women and 50 percent of divorced men say they are better off out of the marriage. Half of divorced adults in the same study report greater happiness. A competent self-help book called *Divorce and New Beginnings* notes the advantages of single parenthood: single parents can "develop their own interests, fulfill their own needs, choose their own friends and engage in social activities of their choice. Money, even if limited, can be spent as they see fit." Apparently, some women appreciate the opportunity to have children out of wedlock. "The real world, however, does not always allow women who are dedicated to their careers to devote the time and energy it takes to find—or be found by—the perfect husband and father wanna-be," one woman said in a letter to the *Washington Post*. A mother and chiropractor from Avon, Connecticut, explained her unwed maternity to an interviewer this way: "It is selfish, but this was something I needed to do for me."

There is very little in contemporary popular culture to contradict this optimistic view. But in a few small places another perspective may be found. Several racks down from its divorce cards, Hallmark offers a line of cards for children—To Kids With Love. These cards come six to a pack. Each card in the pack has a slightly different message. According to the package, the "thinking of you" messages will let a special kid "know how much you care." Though Hallmark doesn't quite say so, it's clear these cards are aimed at divorced parents. "I'm sorry I'm not always there when you need me but I hope you know I'm always just a phone call away." Another card reads: "Even though your dad and I don't live together anymore, I know he's still a very special part of your life. And as much as I miss you when you're not with me, I'm still happy that you two can spend time together."

Hallmark's messages are grounded in a substantial body of well-funded market research. Therefore it is worth reflecting on the divergence in sentiment between the divorce cards for adults and the divorce cards for kids. For grown-ups, divorce heralds new beginnings (A HOT NEW SINGLE). For children, divorce brings separation and loss ("I'm sorry I'm not always there when you need me").

Any event that permanently denies a child the presence and protection of a parent jeopardizes the life of the child.

An even more telling glimpse into the meaning of family disruption can be found in the growing children's literature on family dissolution. Take, for example, the popular 1986 children's book *Dinosaurs Divorce: A Guide for Changing Families*, by Laurene Krasny Brown and Marc Brown. This is a picture book, written for very young children. The book begins with a short glossary of "divorce words" and encourages children to "see if you can find them" in the story. The words include "family counselor," "separation agreement," "alimony," and "child custody." The book is illustrated with cartoonish drawings of green dinosaur parents who fight, drink too much, and break up. One panel shows the father dinosaur, suitcase in hand, getting into a yellow car.

The dinosaur children are offered simple, straightforward advice on what to do about the divorce. *On custody decisions:* "When parents can't agree, lawyers and judges decide. Try to be honest if they ask you questions; it will help them make better decisions." *On selling the house:* "If you move, you may have to say good-bye to friends and familiar places. But soon your new home will feel like the place you really belong." *On the economic impact of divorce:* "Living with one parent almost always means there will be less money. Be prepared to give up some things." *On holidays:* "Divorce may mean twice as much celebrating at holiday times, but you may feel pulled apart." *On parents' new lovers:* "You may sometimes feel jealous and want your parent to yourself. Be polite to your parents' new friends, even if you don't like them at first." *On parents' remarriage:* "Not everyone loves his or her stepparents, but showing them respect is important."

These cards and books point to an uncomfortable and generally unacknowledged fact: what contributes to a parent's happiness may detract from a child's happiness. All too often the adult quest for freedom, independence, and choice in family relationships conflicts with a child's developmental needs for stability, constancy, harmony, and permanence in family life. In short, family disruption creates a deep division between parents' interests and the interests of children.

One of the worst consequences of these divided interests is a withdrawal of parental investment in children's well-being. As the Stanford economist Victor Fuchs has pointed out, the main source of social investment in children is private. The investment comes from the children's parents. But parents in disrupted families have less time, attention, and money to devote to their children. The single most important source of disinvestment has been the widespread withdrawal of financial support and involvement by fathers. Maternal investment, too, has declined, as women try to raise families on their own and work outside the home. Moreover, both mothers and fathers commonly respond to family breakup by investing more heavily in themselves and in their own personal and romantic lives.

Sometimes the tables are completely turned. Children are called upon to invest in the emotional well-being of their parents. Indeed, this seems to be the larger message of many of the children's books on divorce and remarriage. *Dinosaurs Divorce* asks children to be sympathetic, understanding, respectful, and polite to confused, unhappy parents. The sacrifice comes from the children: "Be prepared to give up some things." In the world of divorcing dinosaurs, the children rather than the grown-ups are the exemplars of patience, restraint, and good sense.

Three seventies assumptions

As it first took shape in the 1970s, the optimistic view of family change rested on three bold new assumptions. At that time, because the emergence of the changes in family life was so recent, there was little hard evidence to confirm or dispute these assumptions. But this was an expansive moment in American life.

The first assumption was an economic one: that a woman could now afford to be a mother without also being a wife. There were ample grounds for believing this. Women's work-force participation had been gradually increasing in the postwar period, and by the beginning of the 1970s women were a strong presence in the workplace. What's more, even though there was still a substantial wage gap between men and women, women had made considerable progress in a relatively short time toward better-paying jobs and greater employment opportunities. More women than ever before could aspire to serious careers as business executives, doctors, lawyers, airline pilots, and politicians. This circumstance, combined with the increased availability of child care, meant that women could take on the responsibilities of a breadwinner, perhaps even a sole breadwinner. This was particularly true for middle-class women. According to a highly regarded 1977 study by the Carnegie Council on Children, "The greater availability of jobs for women means that more middle-class children today survive their parents' divorce without a catastrophic plunge into poverty."

Feminists, who had long argued that the path to greater equality for women lay in the world of work outside the home, endorsed this assumption. In fact, for many, economic independence was a stepping-stone toward freedom from both men and marriage. As women began to earn their own money, they were less dependent on men or marriage, and marriage diminished in importance. In Gloria Steinem's memorable words, "A woman without a man is like a fish without a bicycle."

This assumption also gained momentum as the meaning of work

changed for women. Increasingly, work had an expressive as well as an economic dimension: being a working mother not only gave you an income but also made you more interesting and fulfilled than a stay-at-home mother. Consequently, the optimistic economic scenario was driven by a cultural imperative. Women would achieve financial independence because, culturally as well as economically, it was the right thing to do.

The second assumption was that family disruption would not cause lasting harm to children and could actually enrich their lives. *Creative Divorce: A New Opportunity for Personal Growth*, a popular book of the seventies, spoke confidently to this point: "Children can survive any family crisis without permanent damage—and grow as human beings in the process. . . ." Moreover, single-parent and stepparent families created a more extensive kinship network than the nuclear family. This network would envelop children in a web of warm and supportive relationships. "Belonging to a stepfamily means there are more people in your life," a children's book published in 1982 notes. "More sisters and brothers, including the step ones. More people you think of as grandparents and aunts and uncles. More cousins. More neighbors and friends. . . . Getting to know and like so many people (and having them like you) is one of the best parts of what being in a stepfamily . . . is all about."

The third assumption was that the new diversity in family structure would make America a better place. Just as the nation has been strengthened by the diversity of its ethnic and racial groups, so it would be strengthened by diverse family forms. The emergence of these brave new families was but the latest chapter in the saga of American pluralism.

Another version of the diversity argument stated that the real problem was not family disruption itself but the stigma still attached to these emergent family forms. This lingering stigma placed children at psychological risk, making them feel ashamed or different; as the ranks of single-parent and stepparent families grew, children would feel normal and good about themselves.

These assumptions continue to be appealing, because they accord with strongly held American beliefs in social progress. Americans see progress in the expansion of individual opportunities for choice, freedom, and self-expression. Moreover, Americans identify progress with growing tolerance of diversity. Over the past half century, the pollster Daniel Yankelovich writes, the United States has steadily grown more open-minded and accepting of groups that were previously perceived as alien, untrustworthy, or unsuitable for public leadership or social esteem. One such group is the burgeoning number of single-parent and stepparent families.

The education of Sara McLanahan

In 1981 Sara McLanahan, now a sociologist at Princeton University's Woodrow Wilson School, read a three-part series by Ken Auletta in the *New Yorker*. Later published as a book titled *The Underclass*, the series presented a vivid portrait of the drug addicts, welfare mothers, and school dropouts who took part in an education-and-training program in New York City. Many were the children of single mothers, and it was Auletta's clear implication that single-mother families were contributing to the growth of an underclass. McLanahan was taken aback by this notion. "It struck me as strange that he would be viewing single mothers at that level of pathology."

"I'd gone to graduate school in the days when the politically correct argument was that single-parent families were just another alternative family form, and it was fine," McLanahan explains, as she recalls the state of social-scientific thinking in the 1970s. Several empirical studies that were then current supported an optimistic view of family change. (They used tiny samples, however, and did not track the well-being of children over time.)

One, *All Our Kin*, by Carol Stack, was required reading for thousands of university students. It said that single mothers had strengths that had gone undetected and unappreciated by earlier researchers. The single-mother family, it suggested, is an economically resourceful and socially embedded institution. In the late 1970s McLanahan wrote a similar study that looked at a small sample of white single mothers and how they coped. "So I was very much of that tradition."

Each year a million children go through divorce or separation and almost as many more are born out of wedlock.

By the early 1980s, however, nearly two decades had passed since the changes in family life had begun. During the intervening years a fuller body of empirical research had emerged: studies that used large samples, or followed families through time, or did both. Moreover, several of the studies offered a child's-eye view of family disruption. The National Survey on Children, conducted by the psychologist Nicholas Zill, had set out in 1976 to track a large sample of children aged seven to eleven. It also interviewed the children's parents and teachers. It surveyed its subjects again in 1981 and 1987. By the time of its third round of interviews the eleven-year-olds of 1976 were the twenty-two-year-olds of 1987. The California Children of Divorce Study, directed by Judith Wallerstein, a clinical psychologist, had also been going on for a decade. E. Mavis Hetherington, of the University of Virginia, was conducting a similar study of children from both intact and divorced families. For the first time it was possible to test the optimistic view against a large and longitudinal body of evidence.

It was to this body of evidence that Sara McLanahan turned. When she did, she found little to support the optimistic view of single motherhood. On the contrary. When she published her findings with Irwin Garfinkel in a 1986 book, *Single Mothers and Their Children*, her portrait of single motherhood proved to be as troubling in its own way as Auletta's.

One of the leading assumptions of the time was that single motherhood was economically viable. Even if single mothers did face economic trials, they wouldn't face them for long, it was argued, because they wouldn't remain single for long: single motherhood would be a brief phase of three to five years, followed by marriage. Single mothers would be economically resilient: if they experienced setbacks, they would recover quickly. It was also said that single mothers would be supported by informal networks of family, friends, neighbors, and other single mothers. As McLanahan shows in her study, the evidence demolishes all these claims.

Single motherhood and poverty

For the vast majority of single mothers, the economic spectrum turns out to be narrow, running between precarious and desperate. Half the single mothers in the United States live below the poverty line. (Currently, one out of ten married couples with children is poor.) Many others live on the edge of poverty. Even single mothers who are far from poor are likely to experience persistent economic insecurity. Divorce almost always brings a decline in the standard of living for the mother and children.

Moreover, the poverty experienced by single mothers is no more brief than it is mild. A significant number of all single mothers never marry or remarry. Those who do, do so only after spending roughly six years, on average, as single parents. For black mothers the duration is much longer. Only 33 percent of African-American mothers had remarried within ten years of separation. Consequently, single motherhood is hardly a fleeting event for the mother, and it is likely to occupy a third of the child's childhood. Even the notion that single mothers are knit together in economically supportive networks is not borne out by the evidence. On the contrary, single parenthood forces many women to be on the move, in search of cheaper housing and better jobs. This need-driven restless mobility makes it more difficult for them to sustain supportive ties to family and friends, let alone other single mothers.

Single-mother families are vulnerable not just to poverty but to a particularly debilitating form of poverty: welfare dependency. The dependency takes two forms: First, single mothers, particularly unwed mothers, stay on welfare longer than other welfare recipients. Of those never-married mothers who receive welfare benefits, almost 40 percent remain on the rolls for ten years or longer. Second, welfare dependency tends to be passed on from one generation to the next. McLanahan says, "Evidence on intergenerational poverty indicates that, indeed, offspring from [single-mother] families are far more likely to be poor and to form mother-only families than are offspring who live with two parents most of their pre-adult life." Nor is the intergenerational impact of single motherhood limited to African-Americans, as many people seem to believe. Among white families, daughters of single parents are 53 percent more likely to marry as teenagers, 111 percent more likely to have children as teenagers, 164 percent more likely to have a premarital birth, and 92 percent more likely to dissolve their own marriages. All these intergenerational consequences of single motherhood increase the likelihood of chronic welfare dependency.

McLanahan cites three reasons why single-mother families are so vulnerable economically. For one thing, their earnings are low. Second, unless the mothers are widowed, they don't receive public subsidies large enough to lift them out of poverty. And finally, they do not get much support from family members—especially the fathers of their children. In 1982 single white mothers received an average of $1,246 in alimony and child support, black mothers an average of $322. Such payments accounted for about 10 percent of the income of single white mothers and for about 3.5 percent of the income of single black mothers. These amounts were dramatically smaller than the income of the father in a two-parent family and also smaller than the income from a second earner in a two-parent family. Roughly 60 percent of single white mothers and 80 percent of single black mothers received no support at all.

Until the mid-1980s, when stricter standards were put in place, child-support awards were only about half to two-thirds what the current guidelines require. Accordingly, there is often a big difference in the living standards of divorced fathers and of divorced mothers with children. After divorce the average annual income of mothers and children is $13,500 for whites and $9,000 for nonwhites, as compared with $25,000 for white nonresident fathers and $13,600 for nonwhite nonresident fathers. Moreover, since child-support awards account for a smaller portion of the income of a high-earning father, the drop in living standards can be especially sharp for mothers who were married to upper-level managers and professionals.

Unwed mothers are unlikely to be awarded any child support at all, partly because the paternity of their children may not have been established. According to one recent study, only 20 percent of unmarried mothers receive child support.

Even if single mothers escape poverty, economic uncertainty remains a condition of life. Divorce brings a reduction in income and standard of living for the vast majority of single mothers. One study, for example, found that income for mothers and children declines on average about 30 percent, while fathers experience a 10 to 15 percent increase in income in the year following a separation. Things get even more difficult when fathers fail to meet their child-support obligations. As a result, many divorced mothers experience a wearing uncertainty about the family budget: whether the check will come in or not; whether new sneakers can be bought this month or not; whether the electric bill will be paid on time or not. Uncertainty about money triggers other kinds of uncertainty. Mothers and children often have to move to cheaper housing after a divorce. One study shows that about 38 percent of divorced mothers and their children move during the first year after a divorce. Even several years later the rate of moves for single mothers is about a third higher than the rate for two-parent families. It is also common for a mother to change her job or increase her working hours or both following a divorce. Even the composition of the household is likely to change, with other adults, such as boyfriends or babysitters, moving in and out.

Family disruption is best understood not as a single event but as a string of disruptive events.

All this uncertainty can be devastating to children. Anyone who knows children knows that they are deeply conservative creatures. They like things to stay the same. So pronounced is this tendency that certain children have been known to request the same peanut-butter-and-jelly sandwich for lunch for years on end. Children are particularly set in their ways when it comes to family, friends, neighborhoods, and schools. Yet when a family breaks up, all these things may change. The novelist Pat Conroy has observed that "each divorce is the death of a small civilization." No one feels this more acutely than children.

Sara McLanahan's investigation and others like it have helped to establish a broad consensus on the economic impact of family disruption on children. Most social scientists now agree that single motherhood is an important and growing cause of poverty, and that children suffer as a result. (They continue to argue, however, about the relationship between family structure and such economic factors as income inequality, the loss of jobs in the inner city, and the growth of low-wage jobs.) By the mid-1980s, however, it was clear that the problem of family disruption was not confined to the urban underclass, nor was its sole impact economic. Divorce and out-of-wedlock childbirth were affecting middle- and upper-class children, and these more privileged children were suffering negative consequences as well. It appeared that the problems associated with family breakup were far deeper and far more widespread than anyone had previously imagined.

The missing father

Judith Wallerstein is one of the pioneers in research on the long-term psychological impact of family disruption on children. The California Children of Divorce Study, which she directs, remains the most enduring study of the long-term effects of divorce on children and their parents. Moreover, it represents the best-known effort to look at the impact of divorce on middle-class children. The California children entered the study without pathological family histories. Before divorce they lived in stable, protected homes. And although some of the children did experience economic insecurity as the result of divorce, they were generally free from the most severe forms of poverty associated with family breakup. Thus the study and the resulting 1989 book (which Wallerstein wrote with Sandra Blakeslee), *Second Chances: Men, Women, and Children a Decade After Divorce*, provide new insight into the consequences of divorce which are not associated with extreme forms of economic or emotional deprivation.

When, in 1971, Wallerstein and her colleagues set out to conduct clinical interviews with 131 children from the San Francisco area, they thought they were embarking on a short-term study. Most experts believed that divorce was like a bad cold. There was a phase of acute discomfort, and then a short recovery phase. According to the conventional wisdom, kids would be back on their feet in no time at all. Yet when Wallerstein met these children for a second interview more than a year later, she was amazed to discover that there had been no miraculous recovery. In fact, the children seemed to be doing worse.

The news that children did not "get over" divorce was not particularly welcome at the time. Wallerstein recalls, "We got angry letters from therapists, parents, and lawyers saying we were undoubtedly wrong. They said children are really much better off being released from an unhappy marriage. Divorce, they said, is a liberating experience." One of the main results of the California study was to overturn this optimistic view. In Wallerstein's cautionary words, "Divorce is deceptive. Legally it is a single event, but psychologically it is a chain—sometimes a never-ending chain—of events, re-locations, and radically shifting relationships strung through time, a process that forever changes the lives of the people involved."

Survey after survey shows that Americans are less inclined than they were a generation ago to value sexual fidelity, lifelong marriage, and parenthood as worthwhile personal goals.

Five years after divorce more than a third of the children experienced moderate or severe depression. At ten years a significant number of the now young men and women appeared to be troubled, drifting, and un-derachieving. At fifteen years many of the thirtyish adults were struggling to establish strong love relationships of their own. In short, far from re-covering from their parents' divorce, a significant percentage of these grownups were still suffering from its effects. In fact, according to Waller-stein, the long-term effects of divorce emerge at a time when young adults are trying to make their own decisions about love, marriage, and family. Not all children in the study suffered negative consequences. But Wallerstein's research presents a sobering picture of divorce. "The child of divorce faces many additional psychological burdens in addition to the normative tasks of growing up," she says.

Divorce not only makes it more difficult for young adults to establish new relationships. It also weakens the oldest primary relationship: that between parent and child. According to Wallerstein, "Parent-child rela-tionships are permanently altered by divorce in ways that our society has not anticipated." Not only do children experience a loss of parental at-tention at the onset of divorce, but they soon find that at every stage of their development their parents are not available in the same way they once were. "In a reasonably happy intact family," Wallerstein observes, "the child gravitates first to one parent and then to the other, using skills and attributes from each in climbing the developmental ladder." In a di-vorced family, children find it "harder to find the needed parent at needed times." This may help explain why very young children suffer the most as the result of family disruption. Their opportunities to engage in this kind of ongoing process are the most truncated and compromised.

The father-child bond is severely, often irreparably, damaged in dis-rupted families. In a situation without historical precedent, an astonish-ing and disheartening number of American fathers are failing to provide financial support to their children. Often, more than the father's support check is missing. Increasingly, children are bereft of any contact with their fathers. According to the National Survey of Children, in disrupted families only one child in six, on average, saw his or her father as often as once a week in the past year. Close to half did not see their father at all in the past year. As time goes on, contact becomes even more infrequent. Ten years after a marriage breaks up, more than two-thirds of children re-port not having seen their father for a year. Not surprisingly, when asked to name the "adults you look up to and admire," only 20 percent of chil-dren in single-parent families named their father, as compared with 52 percent of children in two-parent families. A favorite complaint among Baby Boom Americans is that their fathers were emotionally remote guys who worked hard, came home at night to eat supper, and didn't have much to say to or do with the kids. But the current generation has a far worse father problem: many of their fathers are vanishing entirely.

Even for fathers who maintain regular contact, the pattern of father-child relationships changes. The sociologists Andrew Cherlin and Frank Furstenberg, who have studied broken families, write that the fathers behave more like other relatives than like parents. Rather than helping with homework or carrying out a project with their children, nonresidential fathers are likely to take the kids shopping, to the movies, or out to dinner. Instead of providing steady advice and guidance, divorced fathers become "treat" dads.

Apparently—and paradoxically—it is the visiting relationship itself, rather than the frequency of visits, that is the real source of the problem. According to Wallerstein, the few children in the California study who reported visiting with their fathers once or twice a week over a ten-year period still felt rejected. The need to schedule a special time to be with the child, the repeated leave-takings, and the lack of connection to the child's regular, daily schedule leaves many fathers adrift, frustrated, and confused. Wallerstein calls the visiting father a parent without a portfolio.

The deterioration in father-child bonds is most severe among children who experience divorce at an early age, according to a recent study. Nearly three quarters of the respondents, now young men and women, report having poor relationships with their fathers. Close to half have received psychological help, nearly a third have dropped out of high school, and about a quarter report having experienced high levels of problem behavior or emotional distress by the time they became young adults.

Long-term effects

Since most children live with their mothers after divorce, one might expect that the mother-child bond would remain unaltered and might even be strengthened. Yet research shows that the mother-child bond is also weakened as the result of divorce. Only half of the children who were close to their mothers before a divorce remained equally close after the divorce. Boys, particularly, had difficulties with their mothers. Moreover, mother-child relationships deteriorated over time. Whereas teenagers in disrupted families were no more likely than teenagers in intact families to report poor relationships with their mothers, 30 percent of young adults from disrupted families have poor relationships with their mothers, as compared with 16 percent of young adults from intact families. Mother-daughter relationships often deteriorate as the daughter reaches young adulthood. The only group in society that derives any benefit from these weakened parent-child ties is the therapeutic community. Young adults from disrupted families are nearly twice as likely as those from intact families to receive psychological help.

Some social scientists have criticized Judith Wallerstein's research because her study is based on a small clinical sample and does not include a control group of children from intact families. However, other studies generally support and strengthen her findings. Nicholas Zill has found similar long-term effects on children of divorce, reporting that "effects of marital discord and family disruption are visible twelve to twenty-two years later in poor relationships with parents, high levels of problem behavior, and an increased likelihood of dropping out of high school and receiving psychological help." Moreover, Zill's research also found signs of distress in young women who seemed relatively well adjusted in middle childhood and adolescence. Girls in single-parent families are also at much greater risk for precocious sexuality, teenage marriage, teenage pregnancy, nonmarital birth, and divorce than are girls in two-parent families.

For the vast majority of single mothers, the economic spectrum turns out to be narrow, running between precarious and desperate.

Zill's research shows that family disruption strongly affects school achievement as well. Children in disrupted families are nearly twice as likely as those in intact families to drop out of high school; among children who do drop out, those from disrupted families are less likely eventually to earn a diploma or a GED. Boys are at greater risk for dropping out than girls, and are also more likely to exhibit aggressive, acting-out behaviors. Other research confirms these findings. According to a study by the National Association of Elementary School Principals, 33 percent of two-parent elementary school students are ranked as high achievers, as compared with 17 percent of single-parent students. The children in single-parent families are also more likely to be truant or late or to have disciplinary action taken against them. Even after controlling for race, income, and religion, scholars find significant differences in educational attainment between children who grow up in intact families and children who do not. In his 1992 study *America's Smallest School: The Family*, Paul Barton shows that the proportion of two-parent families varies widely from state to state and is related to variations in academic achievement. North Dakota, for example, scores highest on the math-proficiency test and second highest on the two-parent-family scale. The District of Columbia is second lowest on the math test and lowest in the nation on the two-parent-family scale.

Zill notes that "while coming from a disrupted family significantly increases a young adult's risks of experiencing social, emotional or academic difficulties, it does not foreordain such difficulties. The majority of young people from disrupted families have successfully completed high school, do *not* currently display high levels of emotional distress or problem behavior, and enjoy reasonable relationships with their mothers." Nevertheless, a majority of these young adults do show maladjustment in their relationships with their fathers.

These findings underscore the importance of both a mother and a father in fostering the emotional well-being of children. Obviously, not all children in two-parent families are free from emotional turmoil, but few are burdened with the troubles that accompany family breakup. Moreover, as the sociologist Amitai Etzioni explains in his 1993 book, *The Spirit of Community*, two parents in an intact family make up what might be called a mutually supportive education coalition. When both parents are present, they can play different, even contradictory, roles. One parent may goad the child to achieve, while the other may encourage the child to take time out to daydream or toss a football around. One may emphasize taking intellectual risks, while the other may insist on following the teacher's guidelines. At the same time, the parents regularly exchange information about the child's school problems and achievements, and have a sense of the overall educational mission. However, Etzioni writes,

> The sequence of divorce followed by a succession of boy or girlfriends, a second marriage, and frequently another divorce and another turnover of partners often means a repeatedly disrupted educational coalition. Each change in participants involves a change in the educational agenda for the child. Each new partner cannot be expected to pick up the previous one's educational post and program. . . . As a result, changes in parenting partners mean, at best, a deep disruption in a child's education, though of course several disruptions cut deeper into the effectiveness of the educational coalition than just one.

The bad news about stepparents

Perhaps the most striking, and potentially disturbing, new research has to do with children in stepparent families. Until quite recently the optimistic assumption was that children saw their lives improve when they became part of a stepfamily. When Nicholas Zill and his colleagues began to study the effects of remarriage on children, their working hypothesis was that stepparent families would make up for the shortcomings of the single-parent family. Clearly, most children are better off economically when they are able to share in the income of two adults. When a second adult joins the household, there may be a reduction in the time and work pressures on the single parent.

The research overturns this optimistic assumption, however. In general the evidence suggests that remarriage neither reproduces nor restores the intact family structure, even when it brings more income and a second adult into the household. Quite the contrary. Indeed, children living with stepparents appear to be even more disadvantaged than children living in a stable single-parent family. Other difficulties seem to offset the advantages of extra income and an extra pair of hands. However much our modern sympathies reject the fairy-tale portrait of stepparents, the latest research confirms that the old stories are anthropologically quite accurate. Stepfamilies disrupt established loyalties, create new uncertainties, provoke deep anxieties, and sometimes threaten a child's physical safety as well as emotional security.

Parents and children have dramatically different interests in and expectations for a new marriage. For a single parent, remarriage brings new commitments, the hope of enduring love and happiness, and relief from stress and loneliness. For a child, the same event often provokes confused feelings of sadness, anger, and rejection. Nearly half the children in Wallerstein's study said they felt left out in their stepfamilies. The National Commission on Children, a bipartisan group headed by Senator John D. Rockefeller, of West Virginia, reported that children from stepfamilies were more likely to say they often felt lonely or blue than children from either single-parent or intact families. Children in stepfamilies were the most likely to report that they wanted more time with their mothers. When mothers remarry, daughters tend to have a harder time adjusting than sons. Evidently, boys often respond positively to a male presence in the household, while girls who have established close ties to their mother in a single-parent family often see the stepfather as a rival and an intruder. According to one study, boys in remarried families are less likely to drop out of school than boys in single-parent families, while the opposite is true for girls.

A large percentage of children do not even consider stepparents to be part of their families, according to the National Survey on Children. The NSC asked children, "When you think of your family, who do you include?" Only 10 percent of the children failed to mention a biological parent, but a third left out a stepparent. Even children who rarely saw their noncustodial parents almost always named them as family members. The weak sense of attachment is mutual. When parents were asked the same question, only 1 percent failed to mention a biological child, while 15 percent left out a stepchild. In the same study stepparents with both natural children and stepchildren said that it was harder for them to love their stepchildren than their biological children and that their children would have been better off if they had grown up with two biological parents.

One of the most severe risks associated with stepparent-child ties is the risk of sexual abuse. As Judith Wallerstein explains, "The presence of a stepfather can raise the difficult issue of a thinner incest barrier." The incest taboo is strongly reinforced, Wallerstein says, by knowledge of paternity and by the experience of caring for a child since birth. A stepfather enters the family without either credential and plays a sexual role as the mother's husband. As a result, stepfathers can pose a sexual risk to the children, especially to daughters. According to a study by the Canadian researchers Martin Daly and Margo Wilson, preschool children in stepfamilies are forty times as likely as children in intact families to suffer physical or sexual abuse. (Most of the sexual abuse was committed by a third party, such as a neighbor, a stepfather's male friend, or another nonrelative.) Stepfathers discriminate in their abuse: they are far more likely to assault nonbiological children than their own natural children.

> *Very young children suffer the most as the result of family disruption.*

Sexual abuse represents the most extreme threat to children's well-being. Stepfamilies also seem less likely to make the kind of ordinary investments in the children that other families do. Although it is true that the stepfamily household has a higher income than the single-parent household, it does not follow that the additional income is reliably available to the children. To begin with, children's claim on stepparents' resources is shaky. Stepparents are not legally required to support stepchildren, so their financial support of these children is entirely voluntary. Moreover, since stepfamilies are far more likely to break up than intact families, particularly in the first five years, there is always the risk—far greater than the risk of unemployment in an intact family—that the second income will vanish with another divorce. The financial commitment to a child's education appears weaker in stepparent families, perhaps because the stepparent believes that the responsibility for educating the child rests with the biological parent.

Similarly, studies suggest that even though they may have the time, the parents in stepfamilies do not invest as much of it in their children as the parents in intact families or even single parents do. A 1991 survey by the National Commission on Children showed that the parents in step-families were less likely to be involved in a child's school life, including involvement in extracurricular activities, than either intact-family parents or single parents. They were the least likely to report being involved in such time-consuming activities as coaching a child's team, accompanying class trips, or helping with school projects. According to McLana-han's research, children in stepparent families report lower educational aspirations on the part of their parents and lower levels of parental involvement with schoolwork. In short, it appears that family income and the number of adults in the household are not the only factors affecting children's well-being.

Diminishing investments

There are several reasons for this diminished interest and investment. In the law, as in the children's eyes, stepparents are shadowy figures. According to the legal scholar David Chambers, family law has pretty much ignored stepparents. Chambers writes, "In the substantial majority of states, stepparents, even when they live with a child, have no legal obligation to contribute to the child's support; nor does a stepparent's presence in the home alter the support obligations of a noncustodial parent. The stepparent also has . . . no authority to approve emergency medical treatment or even to sign a permission slip. . . ." When a marriage breaks up, the stepparent has no continuing obligation to provide for a stepchild, no matter how long or how much he or she has been contributing to the support of the child. In short, Chambers says, stepparent relationships are based wholly on consent, subject to the inclinations of the adult and the child. The only way a stepparent can acquire the legal status of a parent is through adoption. Some researchers also point to the cultural ambiguity of the stepparent's role as a source of diminished interest, while others insist that it is the absence of a blood tie that weakens the bond between stepparent and child.

Whatever its causes, the diminished investment in children in both single-parent and stepparent families has a significant impact on their life chances. Take parental help with college costs. The parents in intact families are far more likely to contribute to children's college costs than are those in disrupted families. Moreover, they are usually able to arrive at a shared understanding of which children will go to college, where they will go, how much the parents will contribute, and how much the children will contribute. But when families break up, these informal understandings can vanish. The issue of college tuition remains one of the most contested areas of parental support, especially for higher-income parents.

The law does not step in even when familial understandings break down. In the 1980s many states lowered the age covered by child-support agreements from twenty-one to eighteen, thus eliminating college as a cost associated with support for a minor child. Consequently, the question of college tuition is typically not addressed in child-custody agreements. Even in states where the courts do require parents to contribute to college costs, the requirement may be in jeopardy. In a recent decision in Pennsylvania the court overturned an earlier decision ordering divorced parents to contribute to college tuition. This decision is likely to inspire challenges in other states where courts have required parents to pay for college. Increasingly, help in paying for college is entirely voluntary.

The deterioration in father-child bonds is most severe among children who experience divorce at an early age.

Judith Wallerstein has been analyzing the educational decisions of the college-age men and women in her study. She reports that "a full 42 percent of these men and women from middle class families appeared to have ended their educations without attempting college or had left college before achieving a degree at either the two-year or the four-year level." A significant percentage of these young people have the ability to attend college. Typical of this group are Nick and Terry, sons of a college professor. They had been close to their father before the divorce, but their father remarried soon after the divorce and saw his sons only occasionally, even though he lived nearby. At age nineteen Nick had completed a few junior-college courses and was earning a living as a salesman. Terry, twenty-one, who had been tested as a gifted student, was doing blue-collar work irregularly.

Sixty-seven percent of the college-age students from disrupted families attended college, as compared with 85 percent of other students who attended the same high schools. Of those attending college, several had fathers who were financially capable of contributing to college costs but did not.

The withdrawal of support for college suggests that other customary forms of parental help-giving, too, may decline as the result of family breakup. For example, nearly a quarter of first-home purchases since 1980 have involved help from relatives, usually parents. The median amount of help is $5,000. It is hard to imagine that parents who refuse to contribute to college costs will offer help in buying first homes, or help in buying cars or health insurance for young adult family members. And although it is too soon to tell, family disruption may affect the generational transmission of wealth. Baby Boomers will inherit their parents' estates, some substantial, accumulated over a lifetime by parents who lived and saved together. To be sure, the postwar generation benefited from an expanding economy and a rising standard of living, but its ability to accumulate wealth also owed something to family stability. The lifetime assets, like the marriage itself, remained intact. It is unlikely that the children of disrupted families will be in so favorable a position.

Moreover, children from disrupted families may be less likely to help their aging parents. The sociologist Alice Rossi, who has studied intergenerational patterns of help-giving, says that adult obligation has its roots in early-childhood experience. Children who grow up in intact families experience higher levels of obligation to kin than children from broken families. Children's sense of obligation to a nonresidential father is particularly weak. Among adults with both parents living, those separated from their father during childhood are less likely than others to see the father regularly. Half of them see their father more than once a year, as compared with nine out of ten of those whose parents are still married. Apparently a kind of bitter justice is at work here. Fathers who do not support or see their young children may not be able to count on their adult children's support when they are old and need money, love, and attention.

In short, as Andrew Cherlin and Frank Furstenburg put it, "Through divorce and remarriage, individuals are related to more and more people, to each of whom they owe less and less." Moreover, as Nicholas Zill argues, weaker parent-child attachments leave many children more strongly exposed to influences outside the family, such as peers, boyfriends or girlfriends, and the media. Although these outside forces can sometimes be helpful, common sense and research opinion argue against putting too much faith in peer groups or the media as surrogates for Mom and Dad.

Poverty, crime, and education

Family disruption would be a serious problem even if it affected only individual children and families. But its impact is far broader. Indeed, it is not an exaggeration to characterize it as a central cause of many of our most vexing social problems. Consider three problems that most Americans believe rank among the nation's pressing concerns: poverty, crime, and declining school performance.

More than half of the increase in child poverty in the 1980s is attributable to changes in family structure, according to David Eggebeen and Daniel Lichter, of Pennsylvania State University. In fact, if family structure in the United States had remained relatively constant since 1960, the rate of child poverty would be a third lower than it is today. This does not bode well for the future. With more than half of today's children likely to live in single-parent families, poverty and associated welfare costs threaten to become even heavier burdens on the nation.

Crime in American cities has increased dramatically and grown more violent over recent decades. Much of this can be attributed to the rise in disrupted families. Nationally, more than 70 percent of all juveniles in state reform institutions come from fatherless homes. A number of scholarly studies find that even after the groups of subjects are controlled for income, boys from single-mother homes are significantly more likely than others to commit crimes and to wind up in the juvenile justice, court, and penitentiary systems. One such study summarizes the relationship between crime and one-parent families in this way: "The relationship is so strong that controlling for family configuration erases the relationship between race and crime and between low income and crime. This conclusion shows up time and again in the literature." The nation's mayors, as well as police officers, social workers, probation officers, and court officials, consistently point to family breakup as the most important source of rising rates of crime.

Terrible as poverty and crime are, they tend to be concentrated in inner cities and isolated from the everyday experience of many Americans. The same cannot be said of the problem of declining school performance. Nowhere has the impact of family breakup been more profound or widespread than in the nation's public schools. There is a strong consensus that the schools are failing in their historic mission to prepare every American child to be a good worker and a good citizen. And nearly everyone agrees that the schools must undergo dramatic reform in order to reach that goal. In pursuit of that goal, moreover, we have suffered no shortage of bright ideas or pilot projects or bold experiments in school reform. But there is little evidence that measures such as curricular reform, school-based management, and school choice will address, let alone solve, the biggest problem schools face: the rising number of children who come from disrupted families.

The great educational tragedy of our time is that many American children are failing in school not because they are intellectually or physically impaired but because they are emotionally incapacitated. In schools across the nation principals report a dramatic rise in the aggressive, acting-out behavior characteristic of children, especially boys, who are living in single-parent families. The discipline problems in today's suburban schools—assaults on teachers, unprovoked attacks on other students, screaming outbursts in class—outstrip the problems that were evident in the toughest city schools a generation ago. Moreover, teachers find many children emotionally distracted, so upset and preoccupied by the explosive drama of their own family lives that they are unable to concentrate on such mundane matters as multiplication tables.

In response, many schools have turned to therapeutic remediation. A growing proportion of many school budgets is devoted to counseling and other psychological services. The curriculum is becoming more therapeutic: children are taking courses in self-esteem, conflict resolution, and aggression management. Parental advisory groups are conscientiously debating alternative approaches to traditional school discipline, ranging from teacher training in mediation to the introduction of metal detectors and security guards in the schools. Schools are increasingly becoming emergency rooms of the emotions, devoted not only to developing minds but also to repairing hearts. As a result, the mission of the school, along with the culture of the classroom, is slowly changing. What we are seeing, largely as a result of the new burdens of family disruption, is the psychologization of American education.

Taken together, the research presents a powerful challenge to the prevailing view of family change as social progress. Not a single one of the assumptions underlying that view can be sustained against the empirical evidence. Single-parent families are not able to do well economically on a mother's income. In fact, most teeter on the economic brink, and many fall into poverty and welfare dependency. Growing up in a disrupted family does not enrich a child's life or expand the number of adults committed to the child's well-being. In fact, disrupted families threaten the psychological well-being of children and diminish the investment of adult time and money in them. Family diversity in the form of increasing numbers of single-parent and stepparent families does not strengthen the social fabric. It dramatically weakens and undermines society, placing new burdens on schools, courts, prisons, and the welfare system. These new families are not an improvement on the nuclear family, nor are they even just as good, whether you look at outcomes for children or outcomes for society as a whole. In short, far from representing social progress, family change represents a stunning example of social regress.

The two-parent advantage

All this evidence gives rise to an obvious conclusion: growing up in an intact two-parent family is an important source of advantage for American children. Though far from perfect as a social institution, the intact family offers children greater security and better outcomes than its fast-growing alternatives: single-parent and stepparent families. Not only does the intact family protect the child from poverty and economic insecurity; it also provides greater noneconomic investments of parental time, attention, and emotional support over the entire life course. This does not mean that all two-parent families are better for children than all single-parent families. But in the face of the evidence it becomes increasingly difficult to sustain the proposition that all family structures produce equally good outcomes for children.

Curiously, many in the research community are hesitant to say that two-parent families generally promote better outcomes for children than single-parent families. Some argue that we need finer measures of the extent of the family-structure effect. As one scholar has noted, it is possible, by disaggregating the data in certain ways, to make family structure "go away" as an independent variable. Other researchers point to studies that show that children suffer psychological effects as a result of family conflict preceding family breakup. Consequently, they reason, it is the conflict rather than the structure of the family that is responsible for many of the problems associated with family disruption. Others, including Judith Wallerstein, caution against treating children in divorced families and children in intact families as separate populations, because doing so tends to exaggerate the differences between the two groups. "We have to take this family by family," Wallerstein says.

Some of the caution among researchers can also be attributed to ideological pressures. Privately, social scientists worry that their research may serve ideological causes that they themselves do not support, or that their work may be misinterpreted as an attempt to "tell people what to do." Some are fearful that they will be attacked by feminist colleagues, or, more generally, that their comments will be regarded as an effort to turn back the clock to the 1950s—a goal that has almost no constituency in the academy. Even more fundamental, it has become risky for anyone—scholar, politician, religious leader—to make normative statements today. This reflects not only the persistent drive toward "value neutrality" in the professions but also a deep confusion about the purposes of public discourse. The dominant view appears to be that social criticism, like criticism of individuals, is psychologically damaging. The worst thing you can do is to make people feel guilty or bad about themselves.

When one sets aside these constraints, however, the case against the two-parent family is remarkably weak. It is true that disaggregating data can make family structure less significant as a factor, just as disaggregating Hurricane Andrew into wind, rain, and tides can make it disappear as a meteorological phenomenon. Nonetheless, research opinion as well as common sense suggests that the effects of changes in family structure are great enough to cause concern. Nicholas Zill argues that many of the risk factors for children are doubled or more than doubled as the result of family disruption. "In epidemiological terms," he writes, "the doubling of a hazard is a substantial increase . . . the increase in risk that dietary cholesterol poses for cardiovascular disease, for example, is far less than double, yet millions of Americans have altered their diets because of the perceived hazard."

The argument that family conflict, rather than the breakup of parents, is the cause of children's psychological distress is persuasive on its face. Children who grow up in high-conflict families, whether the families stay together or eventually split up, are undoubtedly at great psychological risk. And surely no one would dispute that there must be societal measures available, including divorce, to remove children from families where they are in danger. Yet only a minority of divorces grow out of pathological situations; much more common are divorces in families unscarred by physical assault. Moreover, an equally compelling hypothesis is that family breakup generates its own conflict. Certainly, many families exhibit more conflictual and even violent behavior as a consequence of divorce than they did before divorce.

Finally, it is important to note that clinical insights are different from sociological findings. Clinicians work with individual families, who cannot and should not be defined by statistical aggregates. Appropriate to a clinical approach, moreover, is a focus on the internal dynamics of family functioning and on the immense variability in human behavior. Nevertheless, there is enough empirical evidence to justify sociological statements about the causes of declining child well-being and to demonstrate that despite the plasticity of human response, there are some useful rules of thumb to guide our thinking about and policies affecting the family.

For example, Sara McLanahan says, three structural constants are commonly associated with intact families, even intact families who would not win any "Family of the Year" awards. The first is economic. In intact families, children share in the income of two adults. Indeed, as a number of analysts have pointed out, the two-parent family is becoming more rather than less necessary, because more and more families need two incomes to sustain a middle-class standard of living.

McLanahan believes that most intact families also provide a stable authority structure. Family breakup commonly upsets the established boundaries of authority in a family. Children are often required to make decisions or accept responsibilities once considered the province of parents. Moreover, children, even very young children, are often expected to behave like mature adults, so that the grown-ups in the family can be free to deal with the emotional fallout of the failed relationship. In some instances family disruption creates a complete vacuum in authority; everyone invents his or her own rules. With lines of authority disrupted or absent, children find it much more difficult to engage in the normal kinds of testing behavior, the trial and error, the failing and succeeding, that define the developmental pathway toward character and competence. McLanahan says, "Children need to be the ones to challenge the rules. The parents need to set the boundaries and let the kids push the boundaries. The children shouldn't have to walk the straight and narrow at all times."

Finally, McLanahan holds that children in intact families benefit from stability in what she neutrally terms "household personnel." Family disruption frequently brings new adults into the family, including step-parents, live-in boyfriends or girlfriends, and casual sexual partners. Like stepfathers, boyfriends can present a real threat to children's, particularly to daughters', security and well-being. But physical or sexual abuse represents only the most extreme such threat. Even the very best of boyfriends can disrupt and undermine a child's sense of peace and security, McLanahan says. "It's not as though you're going from an unhappy marriage to peacefulness. There can be a constant changing until the mother finds a suitable partner."

McLanahan's argument helps explain why children of widows tend to do better than children of divorced or unmarried mothers. Widows differ from other single mothers in all three respects. They are economically more secure, because they receive more public assistance through Survivors Insurance, and possibly private insurance or other kinds of support from family members. Thus widows are less likely to leave the neighborhood in search of a new or better job and a cheaper house or apartment. Moreover, the death of a father is not likely to disrupt the authority structure radically. When a father dies, he is no longer physically present, but his death does not dethrone him as an authority figure in the child's life. On the contrary, his authority may be magnified through death. The mother can draw on the powerful memory of the departed father as a way of intensifying her parental authority: "Your father would have wanted it this way." Finally, since widows tend to be older than divorced mothers, their love life may be less distracting.

Regarding the two-parent family, the sociologist David Popenoe, who has devoted much of his career to the study of families, both in the United States and in Scandinavia, makes this straightforward assertion:

> Social science research is almost never conclusive. There are always methodological difficulties and stones left unturned. Yet in three decades of work as a social scientist, I know of few other bodies of data in which the weight of evidence is so decisively on one side of the issue: on the whole, for children, two-parent families are preferable to single-parent and stepfamilies.

The regime effect

The rise in family disruption is not unique to American society. It is evident in virtually all advanced nations, including Japan, where it is also shaped by the growing participation of women in the work force. Yet the United States has made divorce easier and quicker than in any other Western nation with the sole exception of Sweden—and the trend toward solo motherhood has also been more pronounced in America. (Sweden has an equally high rate of out-of-wedlock birth, but the majority of such births are to cohabiting couples, a long-established pattern in Swedish society.) More to the point, nowhere has family breakup been greeted by a more triumphant rhetoric of renewal than in America.

What is striking about this rhetoric is how deeply it reflects classic themes in American public life. It draws its language and imagery from the nation's founding myth. It depicts family breakup as a drama of revolution and rebirth. The nuclear family represents the corrupt past, an institution guilty of the abuse of power and the suppression of individual freedom. Breaking up the family is like breaking away from Old World tyranny. Liberated from the bonds of the family, the individual can achieve independence and experience a new beginning, a fresh start, a new birth of freedom. In short, family breakup recapitulates the American experience.

Not all children in two-parent families are free from emotional turmoil, but few are burdened with the troubles that accompany family breakup.

This rhetoric is an example of what the University of Maryland political philosopher William Galston has called the "regime effect." The founding of the United States set in motion a new political order based to an unprecedented degree on individual rights, personal choice, and egalitarian relationships. Since then these values have spread beyond their original domain of political relationships to define social relationships as well. Since the 1960s these values have had a particularly profound impact on the family.

Increasingly, political principles of individual rights and choice shape our understanding of family commitment and solidarity. Family relationships are viewed not as permanent or binding but as voluntary and easily terminable. Moreover, under the sway of the regime effect the family loses its central importance as an institution in the civil society, accomplishing certain social goals such as raising children and caring for its members, and becomes a means to achieving greater individual happiness—a lifestyle choice. Thus, Galston says, what is happening to the American family reflects the "unfolding logic of authoritative, deeply American moral-political principles."

One benefit of the regime effect is to create greater equality in adult family relationships. Husbands and wives, mothers and fathers, enjoy relationships far more egalitarian than past relationships were, and most Americans prefer it that way. But the political principles of the regime effect can threaten another kind of family relationship—that between parent and child. Owing to their biological and developmental immaturity, children are needy dependents. They are not able to express their choices according to limited, easily terminable, voluntary agreements. They are not able to act as negotiators in family decisions, even those that most affect their own interests. As one writer has put it, "a newborn does not make a good 'partner.'" Correspondingly, the parental role is antithetical to the spirit of the regime. Parental investment in children involves a diminished investment in self, a willing deference to the needs and claims of the dependent child. Perhaps more than any other family relationship, the parent-child relationship—shaped as it is by patterns of dependency and deference—can be undermined and weakened by the principles of the regime.

More than a century and a half ago Alexis de Tocqueville made the striking observation that an individualistic society depends on a communitarian institution like the family for its continued existence. The family cannot be constituted like the liberal state, nor can it be governed entirely by that state's principles. Yet the family serves as the seedbed for the virtues required by a liberal state. The family is responsible for teaching lessons of independence, self-restraint, responsibility, and right conduct, which are essential to a free, democratic society. If the family fails in these tasks, then the entire experiment in democratic self-rule is jeopardized.

To take one example: independence is basic to successful functioning in American life. We assume that most people in America will be able to work, care for themselves and their families, think for themselves, and inculcate the same traits of independence and initiative in their children. We depend on families to teach people to do these things. The erosion of the two-parent family undermines the capacity of families to impart this knowledge; children of long-term welfare-dependent single parents are far more likely than others to be dependent themselves. Similarly, the children in disrupted families have a harder time forging bonds of trust with others and giving and getting help across the generations. This, too, may lead to greater dependency on the resources of the state.

Since the 1960s Americans have been conducting what is tantamount to a vast natural experiment in family life. Many would argue that this experiment was necessary, worthwhile, and long overdue. The results of the experiment are coming in, and they are clear. Adults have benefited from the changes in family life in important ways, but the same cannot be said for children. Indeed, this is the first generation in the nation's history to do worse psychologically, socially, and economically than its parents. Most poignantly, in survey after survey the children of broken families confess deep longings for an intact family.

Nonetheless, as Galston is quick to point out, the regime effect is not an irresistible undertow that will carry away the family. It is more like a swift current, against which it is possible to swim. People learn; societies can change, particularly when it becomes apparent that certain behaviors damage the social ecology, threaten the public order, and impose new burdens on core institutions. Whether Americans will act to overcome the legacy of family disruption is a crucial but as yet unanswered question.

2

Divorce Harms Children

Karl Zinsmeister

Karl Zinsmeister is editor in chief of the American Enterprise, *a conservative journal of opinion.*

When parents divorce, the children's relationships with their parents change dramatically. Most children of divorce stay with their mother, who becomes both the nurturer and the disciplinarian. Many children see their fathers less frequently after the divorce. These changes lead to poor educational performance, truancy, criminal activity, and psychological problems for the children of divorce.

Originally, notes family historian John Sommerville, marriage arose to create "security for the children to be expected from the union." Yet nowadays "the child's interest in the permanence of marriage is almost ignored." During the divorce boom that began in the mid-1960s, divorces affecting children went up even faster than divorces generally, and today *most* crack-ups involve kids. Since 1972, more than a million youngsters have been involved in a divorce *each year*.

The result is that at some time before reaching adulthood, around half of today's children will go through a marital rupture. Most of these youngsters will live in a single-parent home for at least five years. A small majority of those who experience a divorce eventually end up in a stepfamily, but well over a third of them will endure the extra trauma of seeing that second marriage break up.

The typical divorce

The typical divorce brings what researcher Frank Furstenberg describes as "either a complete cessation of contact between the non-residential parent and child, or a relationship that is tantamount to a ritual form of parenthood." In nine cases out of ten the custodial parent is the mother, and fully half of all divorce-children living with their mom have had no contact with their father for at least a full year. Only one child in ten sees his non-custodial parent as often as once a week. Overall, only about one youngster in five is able to maintain a close relationship with both parents.

Karl Zinsmeister, "Divorce's Toll on Children," *American Enterprise*, May/June 1996. Reprinted by permission of the *American Enterprise*, a Washington, D.C.-based magazine of politics, business, and culture.

Joint child custody receives a lot of publicity (it is now allowed in about half the states), but it remains unusual. In California, where it is much more common than anywhere else, only 18 percent of divorced couples have joint physical custody. Most divorced children still live solely with their mothers.

"For most men," sociologist Andrew Cherlin notes, "children and marriage are part of a package deal. Their ties to their children depend on their ties to their wives." Studies show that remarriage makes fathers particularly likely to reduce involvement with the children from their previous marriage.

Since 1972, more than a million youngsters have been involved in a divorce each year.

Even when divorced parents do maintain regular contact with their children, truly cooperative childrearing is very rare. Most often, research shows, the estranged parents have no communication or mutual reinforcement. As a result, mother and father frequently undercut each other, intentionally or not, and parent-child relations are often unhealthy.

A series of interviews with children of divorce conducted by author/photographer Jill Krementz illustrates this phenomenon. "My relationship with my parents has changed because now my mother does all the disciplining," says 14-year-old Meredith, "and sometimes she resents it—especially when we tell her how much fun we have with Dad. It's as if it's all fun and games with him because we're with him so little." Ari, also 14, confides, "I really look forward to the weekends because it's kind of like a break—it's like going to Disneyland because there's no set schedule, no 'Be home by 5:30' kind of stuff. It's open. It's free. And my father is always buying me presents." Zach, age 13, reports "whenever I want to see my other parent I can, and if I have a fight with one of them, instead of having to take off . . . I can just go eat at my Mom's house or my Dad's."

Other youngsters feel torn in two after a divorce, particularly in cases of joint custody where they must physically bounce back and forth between two houses. "It's hello, goodbye, hello, goodbye all the time," says one father. Gary Skoloff, chairman of the American Bar Association's family law section, explains that "joint custody was going to be a great panacea, the ultimate solution. . . . But it turned out to be the world's worst situation." The lack of a stable home has proved so harmful to children that several states, including California where the practice was pioneered, have recently revoked statutes favoring joint custody.

Fear and loathing of divorce among the young

Children's view of divorce is unambiguous: it's a disaster. In 1988, professor Jeanne Dise-Lewis surveyed almost 700 junior high school students, asking them to rate a number of life events in terms of stressfulness. The only thing students ranked as more stressful than parental divorce was death of a parent or close family member. Parental divorce received a higher rating than the death of a friend, being "physically hit" by a parent, feeling that no one liked them, or being seriously injured.

The "fairy tale" believed by adults, says University of Michigan psychologist and divorce expert Neil Kalter, is that if they simply present new family set-ups to their children in a calm, firm way, the children will accept them. Actually, he says, that "is seen by the kids as a lot of baloney." Among the hundreds of children he's worked with in setting up coping-with-divorce programs for schools, "there are very few who have anything good to say about divorce." "Children are generally more traditional than adults," agrees Judith Wallerstein. "Children want both parents. They want family." If children had the vote, she says, there would be no such thing as divorce.

Indeed, Gallup youth surveys in the early 1990s show that three out of four teenagers age 13 to 17 think "it is too easy for people in this country to get divorced." Go into a typical high school today and ask some students what their most important wish for the future is and a surprising number will answer "that there wouldn't be so many divorces." Young Arizonan Cynthia Coan has lots of company when she says, "as a child of divorce, I cannot help but hope that the next generation of children will be spared what mine went through."

You'll sometimes hear the claim that divorce doesn't hurt children as much as conflict in a marriage. This is not supported by the evidence. "For kids," reports Kalter, "the misery in an unhappy marriage is usually less significant than the changes" after a divorce. "They'd rather their parents keep fighting and not get divorced." Even five years later, few of the youngsters in Wallerstein's study agreed with their parents' decision to separate. Only ten percent were more content after the split than before.

Even when divorced parents do maintain regular contact with their children, truly cooperative child-rearing is very rare.

Contrary to popular perceptions, the alternative to most divorces is not life in a war zone. Though more than 50 percent of all marriages currently end in divorce, experts tell us that only about 15 percent of all unions involve high levels of conflict. In the vast number of divorces, then, there is no gross strife or violence that could warp a youngster's childhood. The majority of marital break-ups are driven by a quest for greener grass—and in these cases the children will almost always be worse off.

Many mothers and fathers badly underestimate how damaging household dissolution will be to their children. A 1985 British study that quizzed both parents and children found that the children reported being far more seriously upset by their parents' separation than the parents assumed. Despite the common perception that the best thing parents can do for their children is to make themselves happy, the truth is that children have their own needs that exist quite apart from those of their parents. One may argue that a parent should be allowed to rank his own needs above those of his children (though this is not the traditional understanding of how families should work). But one ought not cloak that decision with the false justification that one is thereby serving the children's best interests.

Wade Horn, former commissioner of the U.S. Administration for Children, Youth, and Families, illustrates how parents can be deluded in this way:

> Families used to come to me when I was practicing psychology, seeking advice about how to divorce. They would say, "We want a divorce because we really don't get along very well any more, and we understand that our child will be better off after we divorce than if we stay together." Rarely, if ever, did I hear a family say, "We're having conflict, but we have decided to work as hard as we can at solving our problems because we know that children of divorce are more disturbed than children of intact families."

A major reason parents are making this mistake is because that is what some authorities and many ideologues in the cause of family "liberation" have been telling them. "For years experts said, 'Once the initial trauma wears off, kids make adjustments,'" complains psychologist John Guidubaldi, past president of the National Association of School Psychologists. While it's true that kids make adjustments, Guidubaldi notes in the *Washington Post*, "so do people in prisons and mental institutions. The pertinent question is: Are those adjustments healthy? And the weight of the evidence has become overwhelming on the side that they aren't."

Short- and long-term effects of divorce on children

The longer-term effects of divorce on children are something we've learned a lot about over the last decade. Guidubaldi, who orchestrated one of the large studies documenting these effects, concludes from his work that "the old argument of staying together for the sake of the kids is still the best argument. . . . People simply aren't putting enough effort into saving their marriages." Family scholar Nicholas Zill points out that "if you looked at the kind of long-term risk factors that divorce creates for kids and translated them to, say, heart disease, people would be startled."

In the early months after divorce, young children are often less imaginative and more repetitive. Many become passive watchers. They tend to be more dependent, demanding, unaffectionate, and disobedient than their counterparts from intact families. They are more afraid of abandonment, loss of love, and bodily harm. A significant number—in some studies a quarter—say they blame themselves for their parents' smash-up.

A small study conducted some years ago by University of Hawaii psychiatrist John McDermott sorted preschoolers who had been involved in a divorce a few months earlier into three categories. Three out of 16 children were judged to have weathered the initial storm essentially unchanged. Two of 16 became what he called "severely disorganized" and developed gross behavior problems. The rest, more than two-thirds, he categorized as "the sad, angry children." They displayed resentment, depression, and grief, were restless, noisy, possessive, and physically aggressive.

In Judith Wallerstein's landmark study, almost half of the preschoolers still displayed heightened anxiety and aggression a full year after their parents' divorce. Forty-four percent "were found to be in significantly deteriorated psychological condition." All of the two- and three-year-olds showed acute regression in toilet training. They displayed unusual hunger for attention from strangers. Older preschoolers had become more whiny, irritable, and aggressive, and had problems with play.

Wallerstein's study also returned to its subjects five and 10 years later, and the collected results are quite staggering. In overview they look like this: initially, two-thirds of all the children showed symptoms of stress, and half thought their life had been destroyed by the divorce. Five years down the road, over a third were still seriously disturbed (even more disturbed than they had been initially, in fact), and another third were having psychological difficulties. A surprisingly large number remained angry at their parents.

Contrary to popular perceptions, the alternative to most divorces is not life in a war zone.

After a decade, 45 percent of the children were doing well, 14 percent were succeeding in some areas but failing in others, and 41 percent were still doing quite poorly. This last group "were entering adulthood as worried, underachieving, self-deprecating, and sometimes angry young men and women." In addition to their emotional problems and depression, many felt sorrow over their childhoods and fear about their own marriage and childrearing prospects. About a third of the group had little or no ambition at the 10-year mark. Many expressed a sense of powerlessness, neediness, and vulnerability. Most of the ones who had reached adult age regarded their parents' divorce as a continuing major influence in their lives.

It should be noted that the 131 children in the study experienced divorce in what Wallerstein and associates call the "best of circumstances." Most of their parents were college educated, and at the beginning these children were achievers in school. None of the participants was initially being treated for psychiatric disorder. Most of the families were white and middle class; half regularly attended church or synagogue.

Even in families with all these advantages, divorce wreaks havoc among the young. Summarizing her findings on the offspring of broken marriages, Wallerstein has written that "it would be hard to find any other group of children—except, perhaps, the victims of a natural disaster—who suffered such a rate of sudden serious psychological problems." Other long-term studies reach similar conclusions. "Divorce," says psychiatrist McDermott, "is now the single largest cause of childhood depression." Marital disruption, quite clearly, can wound children for years.

A catalogue of behavioral changes

Let's look more specifically at some of the changes in behavior that affect children of divorce. John Guidubaldi and Joseph Perry found in their survey of 700 youngsters that children of divorced parents performed worse than children of intact families on 9 of 30 mental health measures, showing, among other things, more withdrawal, dependency, inattention, and unhappiness, plus less work effort. Divorced students were more likely to abuse drugs, to commit violent acts, to take their own life, and to bear children out of wedlock.

A University of Pittsburgh study in the late 1980s found that there were 30 percent more duodenal ulcers and 70 percent more suicide attempts—both symptoms of serious psychological stress—among children who had lost a parent. In Wallerstein's middle-class sample, one-third of the girls with divorced parents became pregnant out of wedlock, and 8 percent had at least two abortions. Two-thirds of the girls had a history of delinquency, and almost 30 percent of the boys had been arrested more than once.

The National Survey of Children showed that more than 30 percent of the individuals whose parents separated or divorced before they were eight years old had received therapy by the time they were teenagers. Divorce-children are two to four times as numerous in psychiatric care populations as they are in society at large. In fact, more than 80 percent of the adolescents in mental hospitals, and 60 percent of the children in psychiatric clinics, have been through a divorce. And what is being treated in most cases is much more than just a short-term reaction: the average treatment takes place five years after their parents' marital break-up. At the fully adult age of 23, middle-class women whose mother and father had divorced were three times likelier to have a psychological problem than counterparts from intact families, according to a massive multi-year British study.

In the early months after divorce, young children are often less imaginative and more repetitive.

Schooling is another problem area. Children exposed to divorce are twice as likely to repeat a grade, and five times likelier to be expelled or suspended. (Fully 15 percent of all teenagers living with divorced mothers have been booted from school at least temporarily, according to the National Survey of Children.) Even in Wallerstein's middle-class sample, 13 percent of the youngsters had dropped out of school altogether. Barely half of Wallerstein's subjects went on to college, far less than the 85 percent average for students in their high schools. Wallerstein concludes that 60 percent of the divorce-children in her study will fail to match the educational achievements of their fathers.

Children of divorce also frequently have problems with sexual identity. In most studies, boys seem to be harder hit then girls. Preschool boys tend to be unpopular with male peers, to have difficulty gaining access to play groups, to spend more time with younger compatriots and females, and to engage in more activities traditionally considered to be feminine. Young boys tend to be more vehemently opposed to the divorce, to long more for their father, to feel rejected by him, and to feel uncertain about their masculinity. They are more likely than girls to become depressed and angry. Many later have problems developing intimacy, and build lifestyles of solitary interests and habits.

For girls there is a "sleeper effect"—beginning at adolescence, seemingly well-adjusted individuals often develop serious problems with sexuality, self-control, and intimacy. Kalter found higher rates of substance abuse, running away, and sexual activity among girls who had been through divorce, particularly when the father had departed early on. Wallerstein found that a "significant minority" of girls expressed insecurity, anger, or lack of self-respect in promiscuity, some gravitating to older men or a series of aimless sexual relationships. "I'm prepared for anything. I don't expect a lot," said one 20-year-old. "Love is a strange idea to me. Life is a chess game. I've always been a pawn."

Mavis Hetherington of the University of Virginia has found that girls have special problems when their divorced mothers remarry. She has also shown that the pattern of low self-respect and sexual precocity among girls with a divorced mother does not hold true among girls living with a solo mother due to death of the father—apparently it is active alienation from the father, more than his simple absence, that causes the disturbance. This fits well with psychologist Erik Erikson's view that it is less deprivation *per se* that is psychologically destructive than deprivation without redeeming significance.

Wallerstein points out that teenage girls often view their absent fathers with a combination of idealization and distrust.

> The idealized father that the young adolescent girl imagines is the exact opposite of the image that later becomes prominent in her mind as she grows older—namely, the father as betrayer. . . . Because daughters of divorce often have a hard time finding out what their fathers are really like, they often experience great difficulty in establishing a realistic view of men in general, in developing realistic expectations, and in exercising good judgment in their choice of partner.

Researcher Conrad Schwarz has hypothesized that children who are allied only with their same-sex parent (as a girl growing up with a divorced mother would be) tend to hold a chauvinistic and alienated view of the opposite sex. Conversely, he suggests, children growing up with only opposite-sex parents (like boys living with divorced mothers) tend to have problems with gender identity and self-esteem. One study that fits this hypothesis found that college-age women who had experienced divorce in childhood were more prone to see men as unfeeling and weak than counterparts from intact families.

Female children of divorced parents are more likely to choose "inadequate husbands" and to have marital problems of their own. They are substantially likelier to have extensive premarital sexual experience and twice as likely to cohabit before marriage. They are more frequently pregnant at their weddings.

Divorce . . . is now the single largest cause of childhood depression.

And both male and female children of divorce see their own marriages dissolve at significantly higher rates than counterparts who grew up in intact families. Partly this is attitudinal: One eight-year study of 1,300 men and women found that people who had watched their own parents divorce were much more tolerant of the idea of divorce, and that this tolerance translated into increased marital break-up.

The other thing that childhood divorce encourages, of course, is the avoidance of marriage. "My mom got remarried and divorced again, so

I've gone through two divorces so far. And my father's also gotten re-married—to someone I don't get along with all that well. It's all made me feel that people shouldn't get married," 14-year-old Ari explained to Jill Krementz.

Divorces involving children thus set a whole train of losses into motion, transporting unhappy effects not only over the years but even across generations. And not even children fortunate enough to live in stable homes are wholly insulated from the turmoil. As writer Susan Cohen observes:

> Although I am not divorced and live in a conventional nuclear family with a husband and two children . . . divorce has been part of my daughter Sarah's life since she was two or three. Divorce is in her books, on her television programs, in her lessons at school, in her conversations with her friends, and in her questions to me.

Indeed, divorce is in the very air our children breathe—with lasting significance for their later views of love, families, and life.

3

Single-Parent Families Contribute to Violent Crime

Wade C. Mackey

Wade C. Mackey is a professor of anthropology at El Paso Community College in Texas and the author of Fathering Behaviors.

Children raised in single-parent families (especially those in which the mother is the single parent) are more likely to commit violent crimes both as juveniles and as adults than those raised in two-parent families. Statistics show a relationship between increasing rates of violent crime and the rise in divorce and out-of-wedlock childbearing. Reducing divorce and bolstering the role of fathers in families can help reduce the epidemic of violent crime.

The recent upsurge in violent crime in America has received a great deal of exposure in the popular media. News magazines, television specials, and radio talk shows are filled with the accounts of violent crimes, especially those perpetrated by young men. Naturally, politicians, editorialists, and commentators are now busy trying both to explain the causes of the rise in violent crime and to prescribe appropriate solutions.

In all of this we hear again and again the assertion—somewhere between a myth and a canard—that violent crime arises from unemployment among men. A survey of male unemployment rates and rates of violent crime across the fifty states indicates *no* such relationship exists. Violent crime is not correlated with unemployment rates, much less caused by them.

On the other hand, there is a robust statistical relationship between violent crime rates and the percentage of all children born to single mothers: more illegitimacy, more violent crime. Clearly, neither the mothers nor the infants are committing the violent crimes. Men are. Accordingly, efforts to reinforce marriage and fatherhood appear far more important for reducing violent crime than are programs to reduce male unemployment.

Despite the claims by politicians and pundits, the evidence shows clearly that family disintegration is more important than unemployment as a cause of violent crime. Consider the following:

Wade C. Mackey, "Violent Crime: Too Few Jobs or Too Few Fathers?" *Family in America*, May 1994. Reprinted with permission from The Rockford Institute. Copyright 1994, The Rockford Institute; 1-800-383-0680.

49

1. Rates of violent crime The difficulties in assembling national data on violent crime are formidable and interpretations are normally strewn with qualifications. Nevertheless, there is a general agreement that violent crime has escalated substantially within the last few years. For example, from 1987 to 1990, murder was up 13.2 percent, aggravated assault was up 21 percent, and total violent crime was up 21 percent.[1] For the same time period, arrests of minors (individuals less than 18 years of age) for aggravated assault was 6 percent higher and arrests of minors for murder and non-negligent manslaughter was 46 percent higher.[2]

There is a robust statistical relationship between violent crime rates and the percentage of all children born to single mothers.

---

2. Political and media responses Such escalation would be expected to generate public reaction, and indeed it has. But in their response to the upsurge in violent crime, politicians and journalists alike have simply assumed (without proof) a direct relationship between unemployment—a lack of jobs for men—and violent crime. For example, on *This Week With David Brinkley* on November 14, 1993, Governor Mario Cuomo specifically linked the upsurge in violent crime to a lack of jobs. Others, including Jesse Jackson and Clarence Page, have insisted that if violent crime is to be reduced, a necessary, if not sufficient, precondition is the development of jobs for young men.[3] National news magazines and the most prestigious national newspapers (echoed by local newspapers) have all reinforced the assumption that a lack of employment is somehow the cause of violent crimes: more men unemployed, more violent crimes.[4] The nature of the putative linkage is rarely specified, just assumed. Consequently, in a recent story from the *Los Angeles Times Service* reporting on a theory that aggression is biologically predetermined, the writer notes in passing that such a theory challenges longheld assumptions that social and environmental factors—poverty, joblessness, discrimination, lack of education—are the sole causes of crime and violence.[5]

In sum, the argument surfaces again and again in many forms that if more jobs were available, then the rates of violent crime would decline. Usually no evidence is presented to substantiate the argument. The assertion is simply made.

Explaining violent crime

Another facet of American culture circa 1990 that might be considered in explaining violent crime is that of the disruption of the American family unit: men have been systematically removed from homes in which only the mothers and their children remain. It might seem reasonable to suppose that in the absence of a responsible male, young boys would become more prone to engage in violent behavior. While, as is the case with the unemployment-causes-violent-crime argument, this argument can be made without hard evidence, it can also be empirically investigated.

That is, these two distinct explanations of violent crime are eminently testable. Is it the lack of jobs or the lack of fathers which is driving up the violent-crime rate? Accordingly, three sets of data were gathered:

1. Violent crime rates across the 50 states, i.e., number of violent crimes per 100,000 population;

2. Male unemployment rates across the 50 states; and

3. The percentage of all babies born to unwed mothers across the 50 states.[6]

Clear conclusions

Violent crime and births to unwed mothers Across the 50 states, statistical analysis shows that violent crime rates are significantly related to the percent of all births to unwed mothers.[7] A statistically robust 42.9 percent of the interstate differences in violent crime rates can be attributed to the varying levels of illegitimacy.[8]

Violent crime and male unemployment rates Across the 50 states, analysis shows no relationship between male unemployment rates and violent crime rates.[9]

To check for the extent of (any) overlap in the three social indices, the percent of male unemployment was partialled from the correlation coefficient between violent crime and percent of all births to unwed mothers. The correlation between illegitimacy and violent crime was still significant.[10] That is, violent crime rates are strongly associated with percent of births to unwed mothers independent of male unemployment rates.

It is clear that, across the 50 states, male unemployment rates are simply not linked to rates of violent crime. It is also patently clear that neither the single-parent mothers nor their infants are committing the violent crimes: violent crime is a phenomenon performed overwhelmingly by men.[11]

It is well beyond the scope of this brief report to establish the reasons for the link between high levels of illegitimate births and high levels of violent crime. The disentanglement of cause and effect from correlation is always problematic. Nevertheless, the lessening of violent crime seems much more dependent upon strengthening marriage, fatherhood, and the family unit than upon reducing unemployment.

Notes

1. U.S. Bureau of the Census, *Statistical Abstract of the United States: 1989, 1992*, 110th and 113th editions (Washington: U.S. Government Printing Office, 1989, 1992).

2. U.S. Bureau of the Census, Statistical Abstract (see note 1).

3. See *Waco Herald Tribune*, January 1994, p. 15A; *The McLaughlin Group*, 14 January 1994.

4. See *U.S. News & World Report*, 17 January 1994, p. 37; Kathryn A. Pearson-West, "The Last Common Bond," *Washington Post*, 9 January 1994, p. C8; "Jesse's Right, Wrong," *Waco Herald Tribune*, 16 January 1994, p. 14A.

5. See Sheryl Stolberg, "Scientific Studies Are Generating Controversy," *Austin American-Statesman*, 16 January 1994, p. E1.

6. U.S. Bureau of the Census. *Statistical Abstract* (see note 1).

7. rp=.655; p.001. Note that if Washington, D.C., is included as a state in the interstate analysis (N=51), then the correlation between violent crime and percentage of all births to unwed mothers increases to .825; p.001 (2-tailed). If the percentage of male unemployment is then partialled from the relationship between violent crime and percentage of all births to unwed mothers, the correlation is still significant [rp=.818; p.001 (2-tailed)].

8. $(rp)^2$=.429.

9. rp=.187, n.s.

10. rp=.640; p.001 (2-tailed).

11. See James Q. Wilson and Richard Herrnstein, *Crime and Human Nature* (New York: Simon & Schuster, 1985).

4

Single-Parent Families Contribute to the Breakdown of Society

Jean Bethke Elshtain

Jean Bethke Elshtain is the Laura Spelman Rockefeller Professor of Social and Political Ethics at the University of Chicago.

The disintegration of the American family is one of the most serious social developments that has taken place since the 1960s. Families have ceased to be the most basic social unit upon which the rest of society is built. The late-twentieth-century children of single-parent families are growing up violent, uneducated, addicted to drugs and alcohol, and bereft of values. Without solid families, America's children and society are both damaged.

In their November 17, 1993, pastoral message, "Follow the Way of Love," Catholic bishops reminded us that "the family exists at the heart of all societies. It is the first and most basic community to which every person belongs. There is nothing more fundamental to our vitality as a society and as a church for, in the words of Pope John Paul II, 'the future of humanity passes by way of the family'" (*Origins*, vol. 23, no. 25, p. 433).

If one agrees with the bishops in this matter, it is sobering to realize that the status of the family is very troubled indeed. On *every* index of well-being, the quality of life for America's children is declining. Indeed, American children are in peril in part because they are less and less assured of the sustained care, support, and safety that comes only with order and nurturance in their immediate environments. Children are bearing the brunt of a profound cultural shift whose negative features we can now observe and whose continuing costs will last much longer than our own lifetimes. Renewed attention to the declining status of the family, perhaps because the evidence of wreckage is visible to even the most insouciant among us, will help to forestall further destruction.

I have been on the front lines of the family debate, as it is sometimes

Jean Bethke Elshtain, "The Family in Trouble." Reprinted from *National Forum: The Phi Kappa Phi Journal*, vol. 75, no. 1 (Winter 1995), copyright © by Jean Bethke Elshtain, by permission of the publishers.

called, for nearly two decades. It has not been easy. A defense of the two-parent family as a norm, tethered to the need for children to be reared in a situation of trust, intimacy, fidelity, and security, was regarded by many as a nostalgic yearning for the "good old days" and a refusal to consider prospects for dramatic social transformation in favor of ties that are less binding. But we have tried an experiment in loosening up the ties that bind, and it has failed. It has failed our children; it has failed our parents; and it has failed our society.

A high correlation exists between broken homes and a whole range of troubles for children. Three out of four teenage suicides occur in households where a parent is absent. Eighty percent of adolescents in psychiatric hospitals come from broken homes. Tracking studies report that five out of six adolescents caught up in the criminal-justice system come from families where a parent (usually the father) is absent. A 1988 government survey of 17,000 children found that children living apart from a biological parent are 20 to 40 percent more vulnerable to illnesses of every kind. Out-of-wedlock births are nearly 80 percent in some inner-city neighborhoods where family disintegration is most severe, although this figure is on the rise everywhere. Recent reports state that every day in America over 500 children, aged ten to fourteen, begin using illegal drugs, and over 1,000 begin drinking alcohol. Among fifteen- to nineteen-year-olds, homicide by firearms is the third leading cause of death after motor vehicle accidents and suicide. Murder is the leading cause of death for young African American men, and those who kill them are themselves young African American men. These statistics are just one small part of the overall (and increasingly grim) picture.

"Kids Count" study

Let us consider just one additional study reported in the "Kids Count Data Book," issued by the liberal Casey Foundation. The findings of this study support a call for a dramatic change in the way in which we think about the family and its troubles. One widely held view is that poverty is the leading cause of family disintegration, breakdown, and subsequent troubles for children. This assessment has seemed to many of us too simple a picture of what is happening. We have suggested that cultural transformation fuels poverty and other social and economic problems. What does the evidence unearthed by researchers suggest?

This study compares two groups. Typical members of the first group were a young man and woman who completed high school, got married, and waited until age twenty to have a child. In the second group, the biological mother and father did not marry; neither completed high school; and a child was born when the mother herself was a teenager. In the first group, only 8 percent of the children live in poverty. In the second group, fully 79 percent of the children live in poverty. What these figures suggest is that the best anti-poverty program for children is a stable, intact, two-parent family. Changes in family structure over the past generation are strongly correlated with rising rates of poverty among children.

Consider another example. We have known for a long time that divorce under current laws often spells economic hardship, even disaster, for custodial parents and their minor children. Our widespread "culture of divorce" does little to sustain couples through periods of marital turmoil. The current slight decline in the divorce rate is one small ray of hope. More attention must be paid to the post-divorce situation in child-rearing households and, perhaps even more importantly, to rebuilding and reweaving the threads of community to encourage young people to marry before they have children.

Family matters

Assessing why the family is in trouble begins, then, with an insistence on the importance of mothers and fathers to the life of child, church, and community. In light of the undeniable evidence of family breakdown and de-institutionalization, especially the severing of basic parental ties, it is disturbing to continue to read and listen to those who paint a rosy picture of "change" and "readjustment" and who refuse to confront the actual situation in which America's parents and children find themselves. The decline in the well-being of America's children is directly traceable to stresses and strains that undermine the family as an ethical entity that, in the words of political philosopher William Galston (currently on the White House domestic policy staff), "transmits or fails to transmit the beliefs and dispositions needed to support oneself and to contribute to one's community" ("Family Matters," *Christian Century*, 1993).

The family matters because a range of tasks that families undertake cannot be delegated satisfactorily to other institutions. Stable, intact families make a vital contribution to nurturing communities and citizens. More and more, for example, we find teachers complaining that they cannot do their jobs as teachers because frustrated, angry, lonely children behave violently towards classmates and teachers or, alternately, are "clingy" because they lack parental guidance and comfort. This behavior prevents children from working on reading, writing, and arithmetic.

> *Although the family is the locus of private life, it is also critical to public life, to the life of community and civic associations.*

This assessment received support recently as a result of a study comparing parents' and teachers' ratings of more than two thousand children from ages seven to sixteen. The study showed that emotional and behavioral problems have been increasing since the mid-1970s for American children. As Daniel Goldman reports in the *New York Times*, of 118 specific problems and abilities assessed, a significant worsening occurred in forty-five. That significant worsening was primarily in behavioral problems, including withdrawal, immaturity, and overdependency; inability to concentrate or being too nervous to concentrate; aggressiveness, including lying, cheating, meanness to others, destroying other people's things, disobedience, temperamental outbursts, and incessant demands for attention; and anxiety and depression—feeling unloved, nervous, sad, and depressed.

Goldman quotes Dr. Thomas Achenbach, Director of the Center for

Children, Youth, and Families at the University of Vermont, as saying, "It's not the magnitude of the changes, but the consistency that is so significant." Achenbach feels that there are "probably multiple factors behind such a widespread increase in problems." But he cites especially "less parental monitoring of what kids are doing, less time with parents because there are more single-parent families and families with both parents working, and schools are having to cope with noneducational issues, like discipline, making it harder for them to fulfill their basic mission." We come back to the underlying problem, the breakdown of the family, fueling other difficulties. Clearly, although the family is the locus of private life, it is also critical to public life, to the life of community and civic associations.

An unfriendly culture

Here the testimony of parents and experts converges. When parents are asked to tell their version of our discontents, they lament the fact that it is harder to do a decent job raising children in a culture that is unfriendly to families and family attachments. The overwhelming majority of Americans, between 80 and 88 percent, believe that being a parent is much more difficult than it used to be. Pessimism about the decline of family values is increasing, especially among women and among Hispanic and African American citizens. While the discussion among many advocates and policy planners over the past several decades has tended to focus on how to fund child care given the fact that both parents are in full-time work, the grassroots conversation revolves around cultural values. Parents express a pervasive fear that they have less time to spend in the ethical task of child-rearing and, as a result, that their children are succumbing to the values of a culture parents view as excessively individualistic and materialistic.

Let me offer one other piece of testimony, this from a taxicab ride I took recently in Washington, DC, heading from the Capitol to National Airport. My taxi driver was a Nigerian woman who had come here with her family some eight years ago. She told me that she was hoping to return to Nigeria because American culture was destroying her family. She said to me, as I took notes in the back of the cab, "If they don't tidy that mess up, you can forget it. Where there's no family, kids don't have to answer to anybody. America has to tidy this up! All this lack of discipline. The kids get dumped. We can't even salvage our own kids." She went on to tell me that her thirteen-year-old son had been caught using drugs and that her eleven-year-old daughter had taunted her recently, during the course of a disagreement with her mother, "When I'm twelve years old, I'll have a baby and I'll be on my own." My taxi driver witness, shaking her head, said angrily: "The baby becomes the job, then a second baby becomes a promotion. Things are terrible. I'm sure all this was set up in good faith, but now everything seems to be going wrong."

Families and society

The time is surely right to bring together the concerns of parents and witnesses on the street with the evidence and analyses of experts. Both scholarly and public opinion converge on the conclusion that our children are in trouble, and, according to the National Commission on Children, those growing up in single-parent situations are at greater risk than are those in two-parent households for poverty, substance abuse, adolescent childbearing, criminality, suicide, mental illness, and dropping out of school. Why should this surprise us? Families teach us our first lessons in responsibility and reciprocity. Writes Ernesto Cortez, Jr., of the Texas Industrial Areas Foundation Network, in a piece on the Catholic tradition of family rights:

> Families teach the first lessons of relationships among persons, some of which are essential not only to private life but to public life as well. Within the family, one learns to act upon others and to be acted upon. It is in the family that we learn to identify ourselves with others or fail to learn to love. It is in the family that we learn to give and take with others—or fail to learn to be reciprocal. It is in the family that we learn to trust others as we depend on them or learn to distrust them. We learn to form expectations of the others and to hold them accountable. We also learn to hold ourselves accountable. These lessons of reciprocity, trust, discipline and self-restraint are important to the forming of relationships in public life.

This family is not an isolated unit but very much a social institution, nested in a wider context, that either helps to sustain parental commitment and accomplishment or puts negative pressure on fathers and mothers. That pressure obviously takes many forms, and I have mentioned just a few. Being a parent isn't just another "lifestyle choice." It is an ethical vocation. Communities, including churches, should lighten the burden and smooth the path for parents so that the complex joys of family life might rise to the surface and the undeniable burdens of family responsibility might be more openheartedly borne.

Children lost to society in increasing numbers may be a growing phenomenon, and it is one that we must call what it is: a loss, a crying shame. Protecting, preserving, and strengthening family autonomy and the well-being of mothers and fathers is a way of affirming our commitment to the individual and to that democratic society that best speaks to the aspirations of individuals. The rights of persons are fundamentally social. What is at stake in the family debate and our response to it is nothing less than our capacity for human sociality.

We are well-advised, then, to begin with a view of marital commitment in which we all have a stake, as parents, as teachers, and as citizens. Given the troubles confronting families, I would hope that over the next decade in American society we could set aside sterile disputes and get down to the business of confronting the wider crisis of values. This goal seems possible as leading politicians of the right, left, and center concur that the problem of values lies at the heart of the matter.

Intergenerational connections

Let me conclude with what might be called an ethical ethnography on interfamilial relations. In 1982, Dr. Arthur Kornhaber and Kenneth L. Woodward published a book called *Grandparents, Grandchildren*. The story that the authors tell is gripping, alternately tender and dismal. They point out that every time a child is born, a grandparent comes into being. Their book is "about the emotional attachments between grandparents and grandchildren. More precisely, it is about the loss of these attachments and the effects of this loss on children, on older people, and, to a more limited extent, on the generation in between." Children, who are astute about such matters, know that they are grandchildren. Grandparents know that they are grandparents. How does our society help or hinder, sustain or sever this vital connection? In the long view of history, cutting the connection between grandparents and grandchildren is a relatively recent event. Perhaps that is progress. Perhaps it represents a salutary advance in individual freedom and social mobility. Perhaps children are better off if they don't have to negotiate lots of complex, intense relationships.

> *What is at stake in the family debate and our response to it is nothing less than our capacity for human sociality.*

Not so, claim our authors, and they provide evidence from in-depth interviews with three different groups of grandparents and grandchildren: 1) those with close contact with one another; 2) those with sporadic contact; and 3) those with no contact at all. These groups encompassed three hundred grandchildren/grandparents pairings. With the "sporadic" and "no contact" grandchildren, the authors found a sense of "loss, deprivation, abandonment." Children in these two groups were more likely to express bitterness and cynicism about old people in general. They had a stereotypical, even scornful, view of the elderly. The "no contact" grandchildren were especially troubled and troubling. "All we found," the authors write, "was a wound where, the children felt, a grandparent ought to be." Such children drew grandparents as shadowy figures or ugly caricatures. These children did have a notion of a grandparent—but as a maligned, wizened, untrustworthy "old person."

By contrast, the grandchildren with close contact with grandparents told a variety of specific, concrete stories about their grandparents. These children, unlike the "no contact" group, could muster a sense of a future as older people themselves; they had some inkling of a life cycle. As Kornhaber and Woodward put it, for the children who had known grandparents well and had lost them through death, "their grandparents lived on as constant objects, fixed forever as large and compelling, almost 'heroic' figures in their minds." Of course, many of these grandchildren did some complaining about a grandparent's eccentricities, but they were quite specific complaints about a quite specific individual human being, not hazy images of disgusting old people.

Let me offer as an example the testimony of one grandson, Eric Paul Elshtain, offered at the funeral of his grandfather and my father, Paul G. Bethke, September 14, 1993:

> From childhood there are some images: Grampa feeling a bicep, baiting hooks, pulling weeds, driving a tractor, pulling on and off boots. A small collection, here, and generic in the way childhood memories can be.
>
> It takes adulthood and a great, solemn, pedagogical moment like death and its ceremony to arrange those images in a meaningful

way. Gaps are filled in, history paid attention to; new things are dug out of the piles and drawers and boxes of a life's time, and in matching the small, circumstantial evidences of a child with the heavier collecting of being older, a man's life becomes fuller at the moment it is coffined.

When I saw Grampa the last time, in the corridor of the nursing home he spent his final time in, my mother and I walked him to the common room telling him that he'd just seen his family—a large group was visiting that day—and that it was *his* family, *his* doing. "Yes, that's quite a bunch," he said, "that's my gang."

Some of us here can look back and see the history we've made, the gathering of a crowd we've helped along and carefully built. Some of us wait, wishing to do even half as fine a job as Helen and Paul Bethke have done. And now a part of that doing is gone, one Prime Mover has no longer delayed his stay—and his stay, in the small moments of a kid visiting his grandparents in Colorado, to the kind inspections of a thankful, grown grandson—was wonderful, loving, sometimes difficult and, most importantly, filled with the work we must (and hope to) carry on.

But the pressures of contemporary American culture encourage grandparents to sever ties with grandchildren, whether voluntarily and in the name of "not interfering" with their children's lives or involuntarily and often bitterly when their child divorces his or her mate and the grandchildren are taken away.

Our current individualistic social contract mandates detachment. Old and young alike pay the price. This problem is something we must recognize and to which we must give explicit articulation. I have no space to document the social forms that recognition might take as an alternative to contemporary American individualism, but I think I can summarize it in this way, using an old Celtic saying: "We all warm ourselves on fires we did not build; we all drink from wells we did not dig." That is the recognition that familial nurturance helps to provide for children. Without such forms of recognition, we will enter the nightmarish world of Hobbes' social contract where life is nasty, brutish, and short. We will enter a world of pathos captured in the words of one young boy, shuttled about from one foster care situation to another, who said to a friendly counselor who was trying to comfort him, "I am nobody's nothing."

In this society today, every day more American children realize they are nobody's nothing. That is where we are, to our shame and to our peril.

5

Fathers Are Important to Families

David Blankenhorn

David Blankenhorn is the president of the Institute for American Values, a family advocacy organization in New York City, and the author of Fatherless America.

Almost half of America's children live with only one of their parents, usually their mother. The increasing absence of fathers is a serious social problem. Americans should take steps to increase the proportion of families with two married parents.

Married fatherhood is disintegrating in our society. Tonight, 40 percent of American children will go to sleep in homes in which their fathers do not live. This historically unprecedented estrangement of adult males from their children and from the mothers of their children is the most harmful social trend of our generation.

A fatherhood movement

That's the bad news. The good news is that we may be witnessing the emergence of a fatherhood movement, a diverse and expanding group of leaders, organizations and grassroots initiatives, cutting across ideological, political and racial lines, all aimed at reconnecting men to their children.

Consider the signs. As recently as 1993, few policy-makers were calling attention to fatherlessness as a serious crisis. Yet today the issue is widely discussed, as if all of us had suddenly looked around and noticed for the first time that there is an elephant in the room.

In June 1995, Governor Pete Wilson declared in Los Angeles that "fatherlessness is the most urgent social problem in our society." Two days later in Washington, Representative Eleanor Holmes Norton (D-D.C.) similarly concluded that "father absence is probably the No. 1 problem in the country." Do these two leaders agree about much of anything else? Probably not. But they do now agree on this basic point.

Equally interesting changes are occurring in communities across the

David Blankenhorn, "Let's Hear It for Fatherhood," *Los Angeles Times*, November 22, 1995. Reprinted by permission of the author.

country. In Cleveland, the pioneering work of the National Institute for Responsible Fatherhood, led by Charles Ballard, is being expanded to six other cities. In suburban California, there is the Boot Camp for New Dads in Irvine. Rising like a Phoenix from the decay of Southside Chicago is an enormously successful ministry, the Apostolic Church of God, based largely on calling men of the community to higher standards of marriage and fatherhood. Across the country, hundreds of churches and thousands of men are joining the Promise Keepers, a rapidly growing men's crusade aimed at spiritual renewal, racial reconciliation and a "servanthood" model of male commitment to family.

This historically unprecedented estrangement of adult males from their children and from the mothers of their children is the most harmful social trend of our generation.

Does all of this talk and activity add up to something that can properly be called a movement? No, not yet. The activity is still too fragmented and diffuse. There is not yet that sense of spontaneous excitement and explosive demand for change that has accompanied, for example, the rise of the feminist, civil rights and environmental movements.

But if there is not yet a movement, surely there are the seeds of one.

Two challenges

Whether a fatherhood movement develops fully may depend on how its leaders handle two important challenges. First, as elections approach, candidates may seek to exploit the fatherhood issue for partisan advantage. A responsible debate about ideas for reversing the trend of fatherlessness would be a great service to the nation and to a fatherhood movement; a politically motivated bout of name-calling would not.

Also, a nascent fatherhood movement could founder due to disagreements over basic goals. Is the main purpose of such a fatherhood movement to increase child support payments from young, unmarried fathers? If so, the likely strategy will be new paternity identification and child support enforcement programs, including job training and other social services. Is the main goal to give divorced fathers more access to their children? If so, the likely strategy will be mandatory parenting classes for divorcing couples plus new laws to encourage joint custody of children after divorce.

Both of these goals have merit. But neither of them seeks directly to strengthen marriage, the essential foundation for hands-on, effective fatherhood. Accordingly, neither child support payments nor improved divorce procedures can be the animating purpose of a national movement to renew fatherhood. The basic purpose of this movement must be far more radical—nothing less than reversing the decline of married fatherhood and increasing the proportion of children who grow up with their two married parents. The slogan should be: A father for every child.

6

The Harmful Effects of Single-Parent Families Are Exaggerated

Arlene Skolnick and Stacey Rosencranz

Arlene Skolnick is a research psychologist at the Institute of Human Development at the University of California at Berkeley and the author of Embattled Paradise: The American Family in an Age of Uncertainty. *Stacey Rosencranz is a graduate student in Stanford University's psychology department.*

Many critics blame single-parent families for causing poverty, crime, drug abuse, and other social ills. While a correlation between single-parent families and social problems does exist, it does not necessarily follow that single-parent families cause the problems. For example, rather than causing poverty, the increase in out-of-wedlock childbearing may be caused by growing impoverishment in the inner cities. Instead of attacking the values of single mothers, society should focus on protecting children in families of all sorts from harmful social and economic conditions.

What is the root cause in America of poverty, crime, drug abuse, gang warfare, urban decay, and failing schools? According to op-ed pundits, Sunday talking heads, radio call-in shows, and politicians in both parties, the answer is the growing number of children being raised by single parents, especially by mothers who never married in the first place. Restore family values and the two-parent family, and America's social problems will be substantially solved.

Family values

By the close of the 1992 presidential campaign, the war over family values seemed to fade. Dan Quayle's attack on Murphy Brown's single motherhood stirred more ridicule on late night talk shows than moral panic. The public clearly preferred Bill Clinton's focus on the economy and his

Arlene Skolnick and Stacey Rosencranz, "The New Crusade for the Old Family," *American Prospect,* Summer 1994, ©1994, New Prospect, Inc. Reprinted by permission of the *American Prospect.*

more inclusive version of the family theme: "family values" means "valuing families," no matter what their form—traditional, extended, two-parent, one-parent.

Yet Clinton's victory was quickly followed by a new bipartisan crusade to restore the two-parent family by discouraging divorce as well as out-of-wedlock childbearing. The conservative right has for years equated family values with the traditional image of the nuclear family. The new crusade drew people from across the spectrum—Democrats as well as Republicans, conservatives, liberals, and communitarians. Eventually, even President Clinton joined in, remarking that he had reread Quayle's speech and "found a lot of good things in it."

There's nothing new in blaming social problems on "the breakdown of the family."

While the new family restorationists do not agree on a program for reducing the number of single-parent families, they generally use a language of moral failure and cultural decline to account for family change. Many want to revive the stigma that used to surround divorce and single motherhood. To change the cultural climate, they call for government and media campaigns like those that have discouraged smoking and drinking. They propose to make divorce harder or slower or even, as the late Christopher Lasch proposed, to outlaw divorce by parents with minor children. And some have also advocated restricting welfare benefits for unmarried mothers or eliminating benefits entirely for mothers who have an additional out-of-wedlock child.

Focusing attention on the needs and problems of families raising children could be enormously positive. But the current crusade draws on the family values scripts of the 1980s, posing the issue in a divisive way (are you against the two-parent family?) and painting critics into an anti-family corner. Restricting legal channels for divorce, cutting off welfare to unmarried mothers, and restoring the old censorious attitudes toward single parenthood may harm many children and deepen the very social ills we are trying to remedy.

There's nothing new in blaming social problems on "the breakdown of the family" or in making the "fallen woman" and her bastard child into objects of scorn and pity. Throughout our history, public policies made divorce difficult to obtain and penalized unwed parents and often their children. In the 1960s and 1970s, however, public opinion turned more tolerant and legal systems throughout the West became unwilling to brand some children as "illegitimate" and deprive them of rights due others. Now we are being told that this new tolerance was a mistake.

The results of changing families

Most Americans, even those most committed to greater equality between women and men, are deeply uneasy about recent family changes and worried about crime and violence. The new case for the old family owes much of its persuasive power to the authority of social science. "The evidence is in," declares Barbara Dafoe Whitehead, author of a much-discussed article, "Dan Quayle Was Right," which appeared in the April 1993 *Atlantic Monthly*. Divorce and single-parent families, Whitehead argues, are damaging both children and the social fabric. Another family restorationist, Karl Zinsmeister, a fellow at the American Enterprise Institute, refers to "a mountain of evidence" showing that children of divorce end up intellectually, physically, and emotionally scarred for life.

Despite these strong claims of scientific backing, the research literature is far more complicated than the family restorationists have let on. Whitehead says, "The debate about family structure is not simply about the social-scientific evidence. It is also a debate over deeply held and often conflicting values." Unfortunately, the family restorationists' values have colored their reading of the evidence.

Improving children's lives

Few would deny that the divorce of one's parents is a painful experience and that children blessed with two "good enough" parents generally have an easier time growing up than others. Raising a child from infancy to successful adulthood can be a daunting task even for two people. But to decide what policies would improve children's lives, we need to answer a number of prior questions:

- Are children who grow up in a one-parent home markedly worse off than those who live with both parents?
- If such children are so disadvantaged, is the source of their problems family structure or some other factor that may have existed earlier or be associated with it?
- How effectively can public policies promote a particular form of family and discourage others? Will policies intended to stigmatize and reduce or prevent divorce or single parenthood cause unintended harm to children's well-being? Would positive measures to help single-parent families or reduce the stress that accompanies marital disruption be of more benefit to children?

Finally, is there a direct link, as so many believe, between family structure and what a *Newsweek* writer calls a "nauseating buffet" of social pathologies, especially crime, violence, and drugs? In his Murphy Brown speech, given in the wake of the Los Angeles riots, Quayle argued that it wasn't poverty but a "poverty of values" that had led to family breakdown, which in turn caused the violence. The one sentence about Murphy Brown in the speech—borrowed incidentally from an op-ed by Whitehead—overshadowed the rest of the message. Charles Murray was more successful at linking family values with fear of crime. In a *Wall Street Journal* article, he warned that because of rising white illegitimacy rates, a "coming white underclass" was going to engulf the rest of society in the kind of anarchy found in the inner cities. But what is the evidence for this incendiary claim? And why do countries with similar trends in family structure not suffer from the social deterioration that plagues us?

The family restorationists do not provide clear answers to these questions. And the answers found in the research literature do not support their extreme statements about the consequences of family structure or some of the drastic policies they propose to change it.

Of course, it's always possible to raise methodological questions about a line of research or to interpret findings in more ways than one. The perfect study, like the perfect crime, is an elusive goal. But some of the family restorationists seem to misunderstand the social science enterprise in ways that seriously undermine their conclusions. For example, they trumpet findings about correlations between family structure and poverty, or lower academic achievement, or behavior problems, as proof of their arguments. Doing so, however, ignores the principle taught in elementary statistics that correlation does not prove causation.

> *Some of the family restorationists seem to misunderstand the social science enterprise in ways that seriously undermine their conclusions.*

For example, suppose we find that increased ice cream consumption is correlated with increases in drownings. The cause, of course, has nothing to do with ice cream but everything to do with the weather: people swim more and eat more ice cream in the summer. Similarly, single parenthood may be correlated with many problems affecting children, but the causes may lie elsewhere—for example, in economic and emotional problems affecting parents that lead to difficulties raising children and greater chances of divorce. Making it hard for such parents to divorce may no more improve the children's lives than banning ice cream would reduce drowning. Also, causation can and often does go in two directions. Poor women are more likely to have out-of-wedlock babies—this is one of the oldest correlates of poverty—but raising the child may impede them from escaping poverty. In short, finding a correlation between two variables is only a starting point for further analysis.

The social science research itself is also plagued by methodological problems. Most available studies of divorce, for example, are based on well-educated white families; some are based on families who have sought clinical help or become embroiled in legal conflict. Such families may hardly be representative. Comparing one study with one another is notoriously difficult because they use different measures to assess children of different ages after differing periods have elapsed since the divorce. Some studies, such as Judith Wallerstein's widely cited work on the harm of divorce reported in the 1989 book *Second Chances* by Wallerstein and Sandra Blakeslee, use no comparison groups at all. Others compare divorced families with intact families—both happy and unhappy—when a more appropriate comparison would be with couples that are unhappily married.

In addition, the family restorationists and some researchers lump together children of divorce and children whose parents never married. Yet never-married mothers are generally younger, poorer, and less educated than divorced mothers. And by some measures children living with never-married mothers are worse off than those living in divorced families.

A simplistic picture

The restorationists paint a far darker and more simplistic picture of the impact of divorce on children than does the research literature. Researchers agree that around the time their parents separate almost all children go through a period of distress. Within two or three years, most have recovered. The great majority of children of divorce do not appear to be impaired in their development. While some children do suffer lasting harm, the family restorationists exaggerate the extent and prevalence of long-term effects. For example, they may state that children of divorce face twice or three times the psychological risk of children in intact families. But the doubling of a risk may mean an increase from 2 to 4 percent, 10 to 20 percent, or from 30 to 60 percent. The effects of divorce tend to be in the smaller range.

In fact, a meta-analysis of divorce findings published in 1991 in the *Psychological Bulletin* reported very small differences between children from divorced and intact families in such measures of well-being as school achievement, psychological adjustment, self concept, and relations with parents and peers. (A "meta-analysis" combines data from separate studies into larger samples to make the findings more reliable.) Further, the more methodologically sophisticated studies—that is, those that controlled for other variables such as as income and parental conflict—reported the smallest differences.

In general, researchers who interview or observe children of divorce report more findings of distress than those who use data from large sample surveys. Yet even in the clinical studies the majority of children develop normally. One point that researchers agree on is that children vary greatly in response to divorce, depending on their circumstances, age, and psychological traits and temperament.

The restorationists paint a far darker and more simplistic picture of the impact of divorce on children than does the research literature.

Where differences between children of divorce and those in stable two-parent families show up, they may be due not to the divorce itself, but to circumstances before, during, and after the legal undoing of the marital bond. Most researchers now view divorce not as a single event but as an unfolding process. The child will usually endure parental conflict, estrangement, and emotional upset, separation from one parent, and economic deprivation. Often divorce means moving away from home, neighborhood, and school. Particular children may go through more or fewer such jolts than others.

Researchers have known for some time that children from intact homes with high conflict between the parents often have similar or even worse problems than children of divorced parents. Recent studies in this country as well as in Australia and Sweden confirm that marital discord between the parents is a major influence on children's well-being, whether or not a divorce occurs.

Some of the family restorationists recognize that children in high-conflict families might be better off if their parents divorced than if they stayed together. They want to discourage or limit divorce by parents who are simply bored or unfulfilled. But how should we draw the line between unfulfilling and conflict-ridden marriages? And who should do the drawing?

High-conflict marriages are not necessarily violent or even dramatically quarrelsome like the couple in Edward Albee's *Who's Afraid of Virginia Woolf?* One major recent study operationally defined a high-conflict family as one in which a spouse said the marriage was "not too happy" or the couple had arguments about five out of nine topics, including money, sex, chores, and in-laws. A number of recent studies do show that even moderate levels of marital dissatisfaction can have a detrimental effect on the quality of parenting.

A number of recent studies do show that even moderate levels of marital dissatisfaction can have a detrimental effect on the quality of parenting.

The most critical factor in a child's well-being in any form of family is a close, nurturant relationship with at least one parent. For most children of divorce, this means the mother. Her ability to function as parent is in turn influenced by her physical and psychological well-being. Depression, anger, or stress can make a mother irritable, inconsistent, and in general less able to cope with her children and their problems, whether or not marital difficulties lead to divorce.

Until recently, the typical study of children of divorce began after the separation took place. However, two important studies—one directed by Jack Block and another by Andrew Cherlin—examined data on children long before their parents divorced. These studies found that child problems usually attributed to the divorce could be seen months and even years earlier. Usually, these results are assumed to reflect the impact of family conflict on children. But in a recent book analyzing divorce trends around the world, William I. Goode offers another possibility:

> The research not only shows that many of the so-called effects of divorce were present before the marriage, but suggests an even more radical hypothesis: in at least a sizeable number of families the problems that children generate may create parental conflict and thereby increase the likelihood of divorce.

Never-married single mothers

The problems of never-married single mothers and their children set off some of today's hottest buttons—sex, gender, race, and welfare. Dan Quayle's attack on Murphy Brown confused the issue. It is true that more single, educated, middle-class women are having children. The rate nearly tripled between 1984 and 1994 among women in professional or managerial occupations. But despite this increase, only 8 percent of professional-status women are never-married, Murphy Brown mothers. Out-of-wedlock births continue to be far more prevalent among the less educated, the poor, and racial minorities.

Most people take the correlation between single parenthood and poverty as proof of a causal relation between the two. But the story is more complex. In his book *America's Children*, Donald Hernandez of the Census Bureau shows that if we take into account the income of fathers in divorced and unwed families, the increase in single mothers since 1959 probably accounts for only 2 to 4 percentage points of today's childhood poverty rates. As Kristen Luker has pointed out ("Dubious Conceptions: The Controversy Over Teen Pregnancy," *The American Prospect*, no. 5, Spring 1991), the assumption that early childbearing causes poverty and school dropouts is backward; these conditions are as much cause as effect.

Elijah Anderson, Linda Burton, William Julius Wilson, and other urban sociologists have shown the causal connections linking economic conditions and racial stigma with out-of-wedlock births and the prevalence of single-mother families in the inner cities. Cut off from the rest of society, with little or no hope of stable, family-supporting jobs, young men prove their manhood through an "oppositional culture" based on machismo and sexual prowess. Young women, with little hope of either a husband or economic independence, drift into early sexual relationships, pregnancy, and childbirth.

Middle-class families have also been shaken by economic change. The family restorationists, however, have little to say about the impact of economic forces on families. In her *Atlantic* article, Whitehead mentions—almost as an afterthought—that the loss of good jobs has deprived high school graduates across the country as well as inner-city young people of the ability to support families. "Improving job opportunities for young men," she writes, "would enhance their ability and presumably their willingness to form lasting marriages." Yet these considerations do not affect the main thrust of her arguments supporting Quayle's contention that the poor suffer from a "poverty of values."

The assumption that early childbearing causes poverty and school dropouts is backward; these conditions are as much cause as effect.

There is no shortage of evidence on the impact of economic hardship on families. The studies of ghetto problems have their counterparts in a spate of recent books about other groups.[1] Much quantitative research reinforces these analyses. As Glen Elder and others have found, using data from the Great Depression to the 1980s, economic conditions such as unemployment are linked to children's problems through their parent's emotional states. Economic stress often leads to depression and demoralization, which in turn lead to marital conflict and such problems in child-raising as harsh discipline, angry outbursts, and rejection. Child abuse and neglect as well as alcoholism and drug use increase with economic stress.

New research has confirmed earlier findings that poverty and inadequate income are major threats to children's well-being and development. Poverty has a deep impact because it affects not only the parent's psychological functioning but is linked to poor health and nutrition in parents and children, impaired readiness for education, bad housing, the stress of dangerous neighborhoods, and poor schools as well as the stigma of being poor. One recent study comparing black and white children across income levels found that family income and poverty were powerful determinants of children's cognitive development and behavior, controlling for other differences such as family structure and maternal schooling.

Child poverty in the United States, as the family restorationists point out, is higher than it was two decades ago among whites as well as blacks. It is also much higher in the United States than in other Western countries. But it is not an unalterable fact of nature that children born to single mothers have to grow up in poverty. Whereas our policies express disapproval of the parents, the policies of other Western countries support the well-being of the children.

Larger questions

The family structure debate raises larger questions about the changes in family, gender, and sexuality since the 1960s—what to think about them, what language to use in talking about them. The language of moral decay will not suffice. Many of the nation's churches and synagogues are rethinking ancient habits and codes to accommodate new conceptions of women's equality and new versions of morality and responsibility in an age of sexual relationships outside of marriage and between partners of the same gender.

The nation as a whole is long overdue for a serious discussion of the upheaval in American family life since the 1960s and how to mitigate its social and personal costs, especially to children. The point of reference should not be the lost family of a mythical past conjured up by our nostalgic yearnings but the more realistic vision offered by the rich body of historical scholarship since the 1970s. From the beginning, American families have been diverse, on-the-go, buffeted by social and economic change. The gap between family values and actual behavior has always been wide.

Such a discussion should also reflect an awareness that the family trends we have experienced since the 1960s are not unique. Every other Western country has experienced similar changes in women's roles and family structure. The trends are rooted in the development of the advanced industrial societies. As Andrew Cherlin puts it, "We can no more keep wives at home or slash the divorce rate than we can shut down our cities and send everyone back to the farm."

However, our response to family change has been unique. No other country has experienced anything like the cultural warfare that has made the family one of the most explosive issues in American society. Most other countries, including our cultural sibling Canada, have adapted pragmatically to change and developed policies in support of working parents, single-parent families, and all families raising children. Teenagers in these countries have fewer abortions and out-of-wedlock births, not because they have less sex, but because sex education and contraceptives are widely available.

The fantasy of restoration

Sooner or later, we are going to have to to let go of the fantasy that we can restore the family of the 1950s. Given the cultural shocks of the decades since 1960 and the quiet depression we have endured since the mid-1970s, it's little wonder that we have been enveloped by a haze of nostalgia. Yet the family patterns of the 1950s Americans now take as the standard for judging family normality were actually a deviation from long-term trends. Since the nineteenth century, the age at marriage, divorce rate, and women's labor force participation had been rising. In the 1950s however, the age of marriage declined, the divorce rate leveled off, the proportion of the population married reached a new high, and the American birth rate approached that of India. After the 1950s, the long-term historical trends resumed.

Most of us would not want to reverse all the trends that have helped to transform family life—declining mortality rates, rising educational levels for both men and women, reliable contraception, and greater opportunities for women. Barring a major cataclysm, the changes in family life are now too deeply woven into American lives to be reversed by "just say no" campaigns or even by the kinds of changes in divorce and welfare laws that the restorationists propose.

> *Whereas our policies express disapproval of the parents, the policies of other Western countries support the well-being of the children.*

The task is to buffer children and families from the effects of these trends. Arguing for systematic economic reform in *Mother Jones*, John Judis writes that between the new economic realities and the kinds of broad measures needed to address them, there is "a yawning gulf of politics and ideology into which even the most well-meaning and intelligently conceived policy can tumble." A similar gulf lies between the new realities of American family life and the policies needed to address them.

Yet the potential for ameliorative reform may be greater than it now appears. As E.J. Dionne has pointed out, the debate is more polarized than the public. The 1992 Democratic convention showed how an inclusive pro-family message could be articulated and combined with proposals for economic and social reform. Such a message, recognizing both the diversity of family life and the continuing importance of family, appealed to a broad cross section of Americans. It continues to make more sense and offer more hope than the punitive and coercive prescriptions of the family restorationists.

Notes

1. John E. Schwarz and Thomas J. Volgy's *The Forgotten Americans* portrays the fast growing population of working poor, people who "play by the rules" but remain below the poverty line. Lillian Rubin's *Families on the Fault Line* documents the impact on working-class families of the decline of well-paying manufacturing jobs. Katherine Newman's ethnographic studies, *Falling from Grace* and *Declining Fortunes*, document the effects of downward mobility in middle-class families.

7

Single-Parent Families Have Been Unfairly Stigmatized

Iris Marion Young

Iris Marion Young is the author of Justice and the Politics of Difference.

Some social scientists and politicians have concluded that only traditional two-parent families are capable of raising children successfully. They blame single mothers—both divorced and never-married—for a variety of social problems that are beyond their control. Since there is little conclusive evidence that single-parent families are harmful, society should stop stigmatizing families headed by single mothers and give them the support they need.

When Dan Quayle denounced Murphy Brown for having a baby without a husband in May 1992, most liberals and leftists recognized it for the ploy it was: a Republican attempt to win an election by an irrational appeal to "tradition" and "order." To their credit, American voters did not take the bait. The Clinton campaign successfully turned the family values rhetoric against the GOP by pointing to George Bush's veto of the Family and Medical Leave Act and by linking family well-being to economic prosperity.

Two-parent families

Nonetheless, family values rhetoric has survived the election. Particularly disturbing is the fact that the refrain has been joined by people who, by most measures, should be called liberals, but who can accept only the two-parent heterosexual family. Communitarians are leading the liberal chorus denouncing divorce and single motherhood. In *The Spirit of Community*, Amitai Etzioni calls for social measures to privilege two-parent families and encourage parents to take care of young children at home. Etzioni is joined by political theorist William Galston—currently White House adviser on domestic policy—in supporting policies that will make divorce more difficult. Jean Bethke Elshtain is another example of a social liberal—that is, someone who believes in state regulation of business, redistributive economic policies, religious toleration and broad principles

Iris Marion Young, "Making Single Motherhood Normal," *Dissent*, Winter 1994. Reprinted by permission of *Dissent*.

of free speech—who argues that not all kinds of families should be considered equal from the point of view of social policy or moral education. William Julius Wilson, another academic who has been close to Democratic party policy makers, considers out-of-wedlock birth to be a symptom of social pathology and promotes marriage as one solution to problems of urban black poverty.

Although those using family values rhetoric rarely mention gays and lesbians, this celebration of stable marriage is hardly good news for gay and lesbian efforts to win legitimacy for their lives and relationships. But I am concerned here with the implications of family values rhetoric for another despised and discriminated-against group: single mothers. Celebrating marriage brings a renewed stigmatization of these women, and makes them scapegoats for social ills of which they are often the most serious victims. The only antidote to this injustice is for public policy to regard single mothers as normal, and to give them the social supports they need to overcome disadvantage.

Most people have forgotten another explicit aim of Dan Quayle's appeal to family values: to "explain" the disorders in Los Angeles in May 1992. Unmarried women with children lie at the source of the "lawless social anarchy" that sends youths into the streets with torches and guns. Their "welfare ethos" impedes individual efforts to move ahead in society.

Liberal family values rhetoric also finds the "breakdown" of "the family" to be a primary cause of all our social ills. "It is not an exaggeration," says Barbara Dafoe Whitehead in the *Atlantic* in April 1993, "to characterize [family disruption] as a central cause of many of our most vexing social problems, including poverty, crime, and declining school performance." Etzioni lays our worst social problems at the door of self-indulgent divorced or never-married parents. "Gang warfare in the streets, massive drug abuse, a poorly committed workforce, and a strong sense of entitlement and a weak sense of responsibility are, to a large extent, the product of poor parenting." Similarly, Galston attributes fearsome social consequences to divorce and single parenthood. "The consequences of family failure affect society at large. We all pay for systems of welfare, criminal justice, and incarceration, as well as for physical and mental disability; we are all made poorer by the inability or unwillingness of young adults to become contributing members of society; we all suffer if our society is unsafe and divided."

A simplistic explanation

Reductionism in the physical sciences has faced such devastating criticism that few serious physicists would endorse a theory that traced a one-way causal relationship between the behavior of a particular sort of atom and, say, an earthquake. Real-world physical phenomena are understood to have many mutually conditioning forces. Yet here we have otherwise subtle and intelligent people putting forward the most absurd social reductionism. In this simplistic model of society, the family is the most basic unit, the first cause that is itself uncaused. Through that magical process called socialization, families cause the attitudes, dispositions, and capacities of individual children who in turn as adults cause political and economic institutions to work or not work.

The great and dangerous fallacy in this imagery, of course, is its implicit assumption that non-familial social processes do not cause family conditions. How do single-mother families "cause" poverty, for example? Any sensible look at some of these families shows us that poverty is a cause of their difficulties and failures. Doesn't it make sense to trace some of the conflicts that motivate divorce to the structure of work or to the lack of work? And what about all the causal influences on families and children over which parents have very little control—peer groups, dilapidated and understaffed schools, consumer culture, television and movie imagery, lack of investment in neighborhoods, cutbacks in public services? Families unprotected by wide networks of supportive institutions and economic resources are bound to suffer. Ignoring the myriad social conditions that affect families only enables the government and the public to escape responsibility for investing in the ghettos, building new houses and schools, and creating the millions of decent jobs that we need to restore millions of people to dignity.

Celebrating marriage brings a renewed stigmatization of [single mothers], and makes them scapegoats for social ills of which they are often the most serious victims.

Family-values reductionism scapegoats parents, and especially single parents, and proposes a low-cost answer to crime, poverty, and unemployment: get married and stay married.

Whitehead, Galston, Etzioni, and others claim that there is enough impressive evidence that divorce harms children emotionally to justify policies that discourage parents from divorcing. A closer look at the data, however, yields a much more ambiguous picture. One meta-analysis of ninety-two studies of the effects of divorce on American children, for example, finds statistically insignificant differences between children of divorced parents and children from intact families in various measures of well-being.[1] Many studies of children of divorce fail to compare them to children from "intact" families, or fail to rule out predivorce conditions as causes. A ten-year longitudinal study released in Australia in June 1993 found that conflict between parents—whether divorced or not—is a frequent cause of emotional distress in children. This stress is mitigated, however, if the child has a close supportive relationship with at least one of the parents.[2] Results also suggest that Australia's stronger welfare state and less adversarial divorce process may partly account for differences with U.S. findings.

Thus the evidence that divorce produces lasting damage to children is ambiguous at best, and I do not see how the ambiguities can be definitively resolved one way or the other. Complex and multiple social causation makes it naive to think we can conclusively test for a clear causal relationship between divorce and children's well-being. Without such certainty, however, it is wrong to suggest that the liberty of adults in their personal lives should be restricted. Galston and Etzioni endorse proposals that would impose a waiting period between the time a couple applied for divorce and the beginning of divorce proceedings. Divorce today already often drags on in prolonged acrimony. Children would likely benefit more from making it easier and less adversarial.

The effects of single-parent families

Although many Americans agree with me about divorce, they also agree with Quayle, Wilson, Galston, and others that single motherhood is undesirable for children, a deviant social condition that policy ought to try to correct. Etzioni claims that children of single parents receive less parental supervision and support than do children in two-parent families. It is certainly plausible that parenting is easier and more effective if two or more adults discuss the children's needs and provide different kinds of interactions for them. It does not follow, however, that the second adult must be a live-in husband. Some studies have found that the addition of any adult to a single-mother household, whether a relative, lover, or friend, tends to offset the tendency of single parents to relinquish decision making too early.[3] Stephanie Coontz suggests that fine-tuned research on single-parent families would probably find that they are better for children in some respects and worse in others. For example, although adults in single-parent families spend less time supervising homework, single parents are less likely to pressure their children into social conformity and more likely to praise good grades.[4]

Much less controversial is the claim that children in single-parent families are more often poor than those in two-parent families. One should be careful not to correlate poverty with single-parenthood, however; according to Coontz, a greater part of the increase in family poverty since 1979 has occurred in families with both spouses present, with only 38 percent concentrated in single-parent families. As many as 50 percent of single-parent families are likely to be poor, which is a shocking fact, but intact two-parent families are also increasingly likely to be poor, especially if the parents are in their twenties or younger.[5]

Family-values reductionism scapegoats parents, and especially single parents, and proposes a low-cost answer to crime, poverty, and unemployment: get married and stay married.

It is harder to raise children alone than with at least one other adult, and the stresses of doing so can take their toll on children. I do not question that children in families that depend primarily on a woman's wage-earning ability are often disadvantaged. I do question the conclusion that getting single mothers married is the answer to childhood disadvantage.

Conservatives have always stated a preference for two-parent families. Having liberals join this chorus is disturbing because it makes such preference much more mainstream, thus legitimizing discrimination against single mothers. Single mothers commonly experience credit and employment discrimination. Discrimination against single mothers in renting apartments was legal until 1988, and continues to be routine in most cities. In a study of housing fairness in Pittsburgh in which I participated, most people questioned said that rental housing discrimination is normal in the area. Single mothers and their children also face biases in schools.[6]

There is no hope that discrimination of this sort will ever end unless public discourse and government policy recognize that female-headed families are a viable, normal, and permanent family form, rather than something broken and deviant that policy should eradicate. Around one-third of families in the United States are headed by a woman alone; this proportion is about the same world-wide. The single-mother family is not going to fade away. Many women raise children alone because their husbands left them or because lack of access to contraception and abortion forced them to bear unwanted children. But many women are single mothers by choice. Women increasingly initiate divorces, and many single mothers report being happier after divorce and uninterested in remarriage, even when they are poorer.

Fine-tuned research on single-parent families would probably find that they are better for children in some respects and worse in others.

Women who give birth out of wedlock, moreover, often have chosen to do so. Discussion of the "problem" of "illegitimate" births commonly assumes the image of the irresponsible and uneducated teenager (of color) as the unwed mother. When citing statistics about rising rates of out-of-wedlock birth, journalists and scholars rarely break them down by the mother's age, occupation, and so on. Although the majority of these births continue to be to young mothers, a rising proportion are to mid-life women with steady jobs who choose to have children. Women persist in such choices despite the fact that they are stigmatized and sometimes punished for them.

Reproductive freedom

In a world where it can be argued that there are already too many people. it may sometimes be wrong for people to have babies. The planned birth of a third child in a stable two-parent family may be morally questionable from this point of view. But principles of equality and reproductive freedom must hold that there is nothing *more* wrong with a woman in her thirties with a stable job and income having a baby than with a similar married couple.

If teen pregnancy is a social problem, this is not because the mothers are unmarried, but because they are young. They are inexperienced in the ways of the world and lack the skills necessary to get a job to support their children; once they become parents, their opportunities to develop those skills usually decrease. But these remain problems even when the women marry the young men with whom they have conceived children. Young inexperienced men today are just as ill prepared for parenting and just as unlikely to find decent jobs.

Although many young unmarried women who bear children do so

because they are effectively denied access to abortions, many of these mothers want their babies. Today the prospects for meaningful work and a decent income appear dim to many youth, and especially to poor youth. Having a baby can give a young woman's life meaning, earn her respectful attention, make her feel grown up, and give her an excuse to exit the "wild" teenager scene that has begun to make her uncomfortable. Constructing an education and employment system that took girls as seriously as boys, that trained girls and boys for meaningful and available work would be a far more effective antidote to teen birth than reprimanding, stigmatizing, and punishing these girls.

Just as we should examine the assumption that something is wrong with a mid-life woman having a child without a husband, so we ought to ask a more radical question: just what *in principle* is *more* wrong in a young woman's bearing a child without a husband than in an older woman's doing so? When making their reproductive decisions, everyone ought to ask whether there are too many people in the world. Beyond that, I submit that we should affirm an unmarried young woman's right to bear a child as much as any other person's right.

There is reason to think that much of the world, including the United States, has plural childbearing cultures. Recently I heard a radio interview with an eighteen-year-old African-American woman in Washington, D.C. who had recently given birth to her second child. She affirmed wanting both children, and said that she planned to have no more. She lives in a subsidized apartment and participates in a job training program as a condition for receiving AFDC. She resisted the interviewer's suggestion that there was something morally wrong or at least unfortunate with her choices and her life. She does not like being poor, and does not like having uncertain child care arrangements when she is away from her children. But she believes that in ten years, with hard work, social support, and good luck, she will have a community college degree and a decent job doing something she likes, as does her mother, now thirty-four.

If teen pregnancy is a social problem, this is not because the mothers are unmarried, but because they are young.

There is nothing in principle wrong with such a pattern of having children first and getting education and job training later. Indeed, millions of white professional women currently in their fifties followed a similar pattern. Most of them, of course, were supported by husbands, and not state subsidy, when they stayed home to take care of their young children. Our racism, sexism, and classism are only thinly concealed when we praise stay-at-home mothers who are married, white, and middle class, and propose a limit of two years on welfare to unmarried, mostly non-white, and poor women who do the same thing. From a moral point of view, is there an important difference between the two kinds of dependence? If there is any serious commitment to equality in the United States, it must include an equal respect for people's reproductive choices. In order for children to have equal opportunities, moreover, equal respect for parents, and especially mothers, requires state policies that give greater support to some than others.

Public policy questions

If we assume that there is nothing morally wrong with single-mother families, but that they are often disadvantaged by lack of child care and by economic discrimination and social stigma, then what follows for public policy? Some of the answers to this question are obvious, some not so obvious, but in the current climate promoting a stingy and punitive welfare state, all bear discussion. I will close by sketching a few proposals.

1. *There is nothing in principle any more wrong with a teenage woman's choice to have a child than with anyone else's.* Still, there is something wrong with a society that gives her few alternatives to a mothering vocation and little opportunity for meaningful job training. If we want to reduce the number of teenage women who want to have babies, then education and employment policies have to take girls and women much more seriously.

2. *Whether poor mothers are single because they are divorced or because they never married, it is wrong for a society to allow mothers to raise children in poverty and then tell them that it's their fault when their children have deprived lives.* Only if the economy offered women decent-paying jobs, moreover, would forcing welfare women to get jobs lift them out of poverty. Of course, with good job opportunities most of them would not need to be forced off welfare. But job training and employment programs for girls and women must be based on the assumption that a large proportion of them will support children alone. Needless to say, there is a need for massive increases in state support for child care if these women are to hold jobs. Public policy should, however, also acknowledge that taking care of children at home is work, and then support this work with unstigmatized subsidy where necessary to give children a decent life.

> *Public policy should . . . acknowledge that taking care of children at home is work, and then support this work with unstigmatized subsidy.*

3. *The programs of schools, colleges, and vocational and professional training institutions ought to accommodate a plurality of women's life plans, combining childbearing and child-rearing with other activities.* They should not assume that there is a single appropriate time to bear and rear children. No woman should be disadvantaged in her education and employment opportunities because she has children at age fifteen, twenty-five, thirty-five, or forty-five (for the most part, education and job structures are currently such that each of these ages is the "wrong time").

4. *Public policy should take positive steps to dispel the assumption that the two-parent heterosexual nuclear family is normal and all other family forms deviant.* For example, the state should assist single-parent support systems, such as the "mothers' houses" in some European countries that provide spaces for shared child minding and cooking while at the same time preserving family privacy.

5. *Some people might object that my call for recognizing single motherhood as normal lets men off the hook when it comes to children.* Too many men are running out on pregnant women and on the mothers of their children with whom they have lived. They are free to seek adventure, sleep around, or start new families, while single mothers languish in poverty with their children. This objection voices a very important concern, but there are ways to address it other than forcing men to get or stay married to the mothers of their children.

First, the state should force men who are not poor themselves to pay child support for children they have recognized as theirs. I see nothing wrong with attaching paychecks and bank accounts to promote this end. But the objection above requires more than child support. Relating to children is a good thing in itself. Citizens who love and are committed to some particular children are more apt than others to think of the world in the long term, and to see it from the perspective of the more vulnerable people. Assuming that around one-third of households will continue to be headed by women alone, men should be encouraged to involve themselves in close relationships with children, not necessarily their biological offspring.

6. *More broadly, the American public must cease assuming that support and care for children are the responsibility of their parents alone, and that parents who require social support have somehow failed.* Most parents require social support, some more than others. According to Coontz, for a good part of American history this fact was assumed. I am not invoking a Platonic vision of communal childrearing; children need particular significant others. But non-parents ought to take substantial economic and social responsibility for the welfare of children.

After health care, Clinton's next big reform effort is likely to be aimed at welfare. Condemning single mothers will legitimate harsh welfare reforms that will make the lives of some of them harder. The left should press instead for the sorts of principles and policies that treat single mothers as equal citizens.

Notes

1. P.R. Amato and B. Keith, "Parental divorce and the well-being of children: a meta-analysis," *Psychological Bulletin* 110, (1), 1991, pp. 26–46.
2. Rosemary Dunlop and Alisa Burns, "The Sleeper Effect—Myth or Reality?—Findings from a ten-year study of the effects of parental divorce at adolescence." Presented at the Fourth Australian Family Research Conference, Manly, New South Wales, February 1993.
3. Nan Marie Astone and Sara McLanahan, "Family Structure and High School Completion: The Role of Parental Practices," Institute for Research on Poverty Discussion Paper no. 905-9; Madison, WI, 1989.
4. Stephanie Coontz, *The Way We Never Were* (Basic Books, 1992).
5. Coontz, op. cit., pp. 259–60.
6. In the work cited above, Astone and McLanahan found that teachers treated children differently if they believed that they came from "broken" homes.

8

The Harm Caused by Unwed Mothers Is Exaggerated

Clarence Page

Clarence Page is a syndicated columnist for the Chicago Tribune.

Society often blames unwed mothers for causing poverty and raising violent and underachieving children. Unwed mothers can raise children as successfully as two-parent families can. The number of parents a child has matters far less than the quality of parenting he or she receives. Teenage unwed mothers should be given help to become good parents and to avoid poverty.

Put the word "unwed" together with "mother" and suddenly you have a convenient target to blame for just about everything that ails modern American life.

Former Vice President Dan Quayle sounded pretty lonely in 1992 when, in a speech about urban unrest, he castigated television's "Murphy Brown" for encouraging the notion that unwed motherhood was "just another life-style choice."

But today he has plenty of company, including President Clinton. "There were a lot of very good things in that speech," Clinton said of Quayle in an interview in November 1993. "Would we be a better-off society if babies were born to married couples? You bet we would."

Yet just the opposite is happening, according to a Census Bureau report on births to unwed mothers, and it is happening in a very dramatic way.

Census revelations

Among the highlights of the census data that made big headlines:

• Birthrates among unwed women soared by more than 70 percent from 1983 to 1993.

• For the first time, children living with one parent were almost equally divided between those whose parents were divorced and those whose parents had never married. Only 10 years earlier, children of divorce outnumbered children born out of wedlock by two-to-one.

Clarence Page, "Census Reflects a Changing 'Family,'" *Liberal Opinion Week*, August 8, 1994. Reprinted by permission: Tribune Media Services.

• Households headed by two parents had incomes four times those of households headed by never-married single parents.

• Blacks bear the biggest brunt of this problem, with 57 percent of black children living with one parent who has never married, compared to 21 percent for white children and 32 percent for Latino children.

Close on the heels of this news came chattering politicians voicing alarm over the breakdown of the family and perhaps the very collapse of civilization as we know it if tough welfare reform is not passed soon.

From the Clinton administration's side came new calls for a two-year limit on Aid to Families with Dependent Children followed by a forced choice between a job or job training or a cutoff of aid. Republicans, guided largely by the ideas of conservative social critic Charles Murray, who believes welfare itself is a principal cause of poverty, particularly for teenaged moms, are pushing for freezing welfare benefits at current levels and denying cash benefits to single mothers under age 18.

No question that we need to reform our welfare system in ways that encourage work and two-parent family life. Homes headed by unwed mothers tend more often than two-parent households to be plagued by poverty, crime, violence, drug addiction, sexually transmitted diseases, poor school achievement and high infant mortality, to name a few ills.

Scapegoating unwed mothers

But as appealing as it might be to make unwed mothers the scapegoats for these problems, it is important to remember a few things:

Most children, whether produced by wed or unwed mothers, turn out reasonably well. Sociological studies that allow for income differences find the success rates between children from single-parent and married-parent households shrink dramatically. It may take a heroic effort, but most single mothers do a reasonably good job of meeting the task.

It is not the quantity of parents but the quality of parenting that counts. A child often is better off living with one good parent than with two parents, one good and one abusive, just for the sake of maintaining a two-parent household.

Second, reducing or cutting off welfare payments probably will not reduce unwed motherhood, since the new reported growth of unwed mothers transcends class lines.

Most children, whether produced by wed or unwed mothers, turn out reasonably well.

Besides, despite the common stereotype of welfare mothers as producers of multiple babies by multiple lovers outside of wedlock, about three-fifths of women who bear a child outside of marriage are not receiving any welfare benefits at all three years after the child's birth. Of those who remain on welfare for longer periods, their numbers have grown despite the steady drop in the value of welfare checks because of inflation since the 1960s.

Unwed motherhood grew among women in all educational levels, but bears close links to poverty. Median family income in households where two parents were present was $43,578, the census bureau found, compared to $17,014 in one-parent homes where the mother was divorced and only $9,272 where the mother had never been married.

That linkage causes some observers to conclude that unwed motherhood is a cause of poverty. Sometimes it is, particularly among teens. But both poverty and unwed motherhood often are symptoms of the same deeper problems.

Unwed teen mothers

The most problematic unwed mothers are teens, a group whose ranks began to grow after the 1950s. Teenage girls who get pregnant tend to be girls who, for some reason or other, have so little faith in their own futures that they don't try very hard not to get pregnant.

It has become fashionable in some circles to blame the morality of the freewheeling '60s for the rise in unwed motherhood, but one could just as easily blame as a root cause the structural changes in the economy that eliminated most of the traditional high-paying breadwinner jobs that young men, urban and rural, used to depend on to support a family. Couple the shrinkage in marriageable men with the tendency of women, wed or unwed, to be channeled into low-paying jobs and you have a recipe for hardship, family stress and moral breakdown.

No, not all unwed mothers are problems, but their problems tend to affect us all.

9

Single Mothers Are Unfairly Blamed for Poverty

Holly Sklar

Holly Sklar writes for Z Magazine, *a monthly left-wing political jour-nal. She is the author of several books, including* Trilateralism: The Trilateral Commission and Elite Planning for World Management *and* Poverty in the American Dream.

According to many social commentators, poverty, along with myriad other social pathologies, is the direct result of the increase in single motherhood, especially among minorities. This view, however, is sexist and racist. The "culture of poverty" that worries politicians and social scientists stems not from single-parent fam-ilies, but from a combination of low wages, exploitation of work-ers, little government support for families, and racial discrimina-tion and sexism that keep minorities and women out of higher-paying jobs.

The reality is that most poor Americans are white, many married cou-ples are poor, and even if there were no nonwhite children and no sin-gle mother families, the United States would have one of the highest child poverty rates among the capitalist powers. But that doesn't stop lib-erals and conservatives alike from blaming poverty on single mothers, es-pecially Black single mothers, and accusing them of breeding a patholog-ical underclass culture of poverty, drug abuse, sloth, and savagery.

In a 1992 speech to Yale University, slandering single mothers and af-firmative action, neoliberal Massachusetts Senator John Kerry recycled the refuted, racist Black matriarchy myth popularized by neoconservative Daniel Patrick Moynihan in a 1965 report released by the White House shortly after the Watts riots: "Twenty-seven years ago, my Senate colleague Daniel Patrick Moynihan warned that: 'from the wild Irish slums of the 19th century eastern seaboard, to the riot-torn suburbs of Los Angeles, there is one unmistakable lesson in American history: A society that allows a large number of young men to grow up in broken families . . . never ac-quiring any stable relationship to . . . authority, never acquiring any ratio-

Holly Sklar, "The Upperclass and Mothers N the Hood," *Z Magazine*, March 1993. Reprinted with permission of the author and *Z Magazine*.

nal expectations about the future—that society asks for and gets chaos. Crime, violence, unrest, disorder—more particularly, the furious, unrestrained lashing out at the whole social structure—that is not only to be expected; it is very near inevitable.'" [ellipses Kerry's] (See *Z*, May/June 1992.)

As films like *Boyz N the Hood* show, you don't have to be a neoconservative (Black or white) to equate Black female-headed families with disorder, savagery, and death and male-headed families with discipline, salvation, and success. Once again, children are stigmatized from birth as the pathological bastards of their mother's presence and their father's absence. Once again, misogynist myths are used to perpetuate racial, gender, and class discrimination.

Mammys, matriarchs, and patriarchy

Culture of poverty theories are neither new nor true, but back they come to mask cultures of greed, racism, and sexism. "It's clear women have been viewed as the breeders of poverty, juvenile delinquency, criminality, and other social problems," says Mimi Abramovitz, professor of Social Work at Hunter College, "from the 'tenement class' of the mid 1800s and the 'dangerous classes' of the 1880s, to Social Darwinism and eugenics, to Freudian theories of motherhood, to today's 'underclass'."

Stereotypes reflect power relations, as some past generations of poor white European immigrants could attest. As Oscar Handlin writes in *Boston's Immigrants*, "the Irish were the largest components of the state poorhouse population and a great majority of all paupers . . . after 1845." They were economically exploited and socially stereotyped as immoral, drunkards, and criminals (recall the term "Paddy wagon" for police wagon). Alcoholism was once recorded as a cause of death for Irish immigrants in the Massachusetts registry, not for Protestant Anglo-Saxons. A century later, Oscar Lewis coined the phrase "culture of poverty," first for Mexicans in 1959, then Puerto Ricans and African-Americans.

Imagine labeling married-couple families as pathological breeding grounds of patriarchal domestic violence, or suggesting that women should never marry, because they are more likely to be beaten and killed by a spouse than a stranger. In Massachusetts during the first half of 1992, nearly three out of four women whose murderers are known were killed by husbands, boyfriends, or ex-partners. Misogynist domestic violence is so rampant that over 50,000 Massachusetts women have taken out restraining orders against former mates. Violence is the leading cause of injuries to women ages 15 to 44, "more common than automobile accidents, muggings, and cancer deaths combined." It is estimated that a woman has between a one in five and a one in three chance of being physically assaulted by a partner or ex-partner during her lifetime. More than 90 women were murdered every week in 1991. In the words of an October 1992 Senate Judiciary Committee report, "Every week is a week of terror for at least 21,000 American women" of all races, regions, educational, and economic backgrounds, whose "domestic assaults, rapes and murders were reported to the police." As many as three million more domestic violence crimes may go unreported.

Stephanie Coontz writes in her myth-busting study of families, *The Way We Never Were*, "families whose members are police officers or who serve in the military have much higher rates of divorce, family violence, and substance abuse than do other families, but we seldom accuse them of constituting an 'underclass' with a dysfunctional culture."

In *The Negro Family*, published the year following the 1964 Civil Rights Act, Moynihan embellished sociologist E. Franklin Frazier's thesis of the Black matriarch in whom "neither economic necessity nor tradition had instilled the spirit of subordination to masculine authority." Moynihan's notion that matriarchal families are at the core of a Black "tangle of pathology" was the perfect divisive response to the Black liberation movement, feminism, and the welfare rights movement.

African-American women have been stereotyped since slavery as "mammies, matriarchs, and other controlling images," explains Patricia Hill Collins in *Black Feminist Thought*. The mammy was "the faithful, obedient domestic servant. Created to justify the economic exploitation of house slaves and sustained to explain Black women's long-standing restriction to domestic service, the mammy represents the normative yardstick to evaluate all Black women's behavior. By loving, nurturing, and caring for her white children and 'family' better than her own, the mammy symbolizes the dominant group's perceptions of the ideal Black female relationship to elite white male power. . . . She has accepted her subordination." While "the mammy represents the 'good' Black mother, the matriarch symbolizes the 'bad' Black mother. . . . Spending too much time away from home, these working mothers ostensibly cannot properly supervise their children and are a major contributing factor to their children's school failure. As overly aggressive, unfeminine women, Black matriarchs allegedly emasculate their lovers and husbands."

Collins notes that the image of the Black matriarch in the post–World War II era was "a powerful symbol for both Black and white women of what can go wrong if white patriarchal power is challenged. Aggressive, assertive women are penalized—they are abandoned by their men, end up impoverished, and are stigmatized as being unfeminine."

Children are stigmatized from birth as the pathological bastards of their mother's presence and their father's absence. historical changes of societal images of woman

---

During World War II, societal images of women changed to reinforce their role in wartime industry. As Susan Faludi writes in *Backlash*: "Rosie the Riveter was revered and, in 1941, Wonder Woman was introduced." Women protested for equal pay and expanded day care and overwhelmingly voiced their intention to keep their jobs in peacetime. When the war ended, so did the supportive images of women workers. Women were abruptly purged from higher-paid industrial jobs and the government shut down its wartime day care services. "Employers who had applauded women's work during the war," says Faludi, "now accused working women of incompetence or 'bad attitudes'—and laid them off at rates that were 75 percent higher than men's. . . . The rise in female autonomy and aggressiveness, scholars and government officials agreed, was causing a rise in juvenile delinquency and divorce rates—and would only lead to the collapse of the family. Child-care authorities, most notably Dr. Benjamin Spock, demanded that wives stay home."

"The backlash of the feminine-mystique years did not return working women to the home," continues Faludi. "Rather, the culture derided them; employers discriminated against them; government promoted new [discriminatory] employment policies . . . the proportion of [women] who were relegated to low-paying jobs rose, their pay gap climbed, and occupational segregation increased as their numbers in the higher-paying professions declined from one-half in 1930 to about one-third by 1960." Faludi observes, "Women's contradictory circumstances in the '50s—rising economic participation coupled with an embattled and diminished cultural stature—is the central paradox of women under a backlash." And backlashes hit women of color the hardest.

"Welfare queens" and worker bees

The third controlling image of Black women, explains Patricia Hill Collins, is the welfare mother. "Essentially an updated version of the breeder woman image created during slavery, this image provides an ideological justification for efforts to harness Black women's fertility to the needs of a changing political economy. . . . Slaveowners wanted enslaved Africans to 'breed' because every slave child born represented a valuable unit of property, another unit of labor, and, if female, the prospects for more slaves." The welfare mother is labeled a bad mother, like the matriarch, but "while the matriarch's unavailability contributed to her children's poor socialization, the welfare mother's accessibility is deemed the problem." Blacks made up a higher percentage of the U.S. population in 1850 than in 1950 or any time in the twentieth century.

In the postwar period, as the percentage of births to unmarried women rose, especially among white women, and Aid to Dependent Children was opened to their offspring, both Black and white women were viewed as breeders, observes Ricki Solinger in *Wake Up Little Susie: Single Pregnancy and Race Before Roe v. Wade.* But white unwed mothers "were viewed as socially productive breeders whose babies" if given up for adoption "could offer infertile couples their only chance to construct proper families." Black women "were viewed as socially unproductive breeders, constrainable only by punitive, legal sanctions. Proponents of school segregation, restrictive public housing, exclusionary welfare policies, and enforced sterilization or birth control all used the issue of relatively high rates of black illegitimacy to support their campaigns." White unwed mothers could be redeemed from their state of "shame" through racially biased government supported maternity homes, adoption, and subsequent homemaker mom/breadwinner dad marriage—which, though rare for most American history, was enshrined as traditional with the help of postwar television.

Black women, explains Solinger, were "simply blamed" for the "population bomb," escalating welfare costs, and giving birth "to Black America, with all its 'defects'." For Black women, "there was no redemption . . . only the retribution of sterilization, harassment by welfare officials, and public policies that threatened to starve them and their babies." As Solinger puts it, "the bodies of black women became political terrain on which some proponents of white supremacy mounted their campaigns" and "the black illegitimate baby became the child white politicians and taxpayers loved to hate."

Aid to Families with Dependent Children (AFDC) expanded for many reasons, among them the inclusion of mothers (and not just their children) as recipients after 1950, higher rates of female-headed households due to divorce and unmarried births, and later the mobilization of poor people in the National Welfare Rights Organization. Black women were "blamed" though only about 16 percent of nonwhite unwed mothers received welfare grants while 30 percent of the unwed white mothers who did not give their children up for adoption received grants in 1959. (In 1960, about 94 percent of Black and 29 percent of white "illegitimate" babies lived with natural parents or relatives.) As Piven and Cloward point out in *Regulating the Poor*, the proportion of Blacks on AFDC rose after 1948 because of two often-neglected factors: the displacement of Blacks from southern agriculture by mechanization and their migration to northern cities (where jobs and low-cost housing became scarcer) and the lessening of eligibility discrimination. While the proportion of AFDC parents who are white (non-Hispanic) was the same in 1973 (38 percent) as 1990, the proportion who are Black declined from 45.8 percent to 39.7 percent in the same period.

The stereotype "welfare queen" lazily collects government checks and reproduces poverty by passing on her pathologies to her many children. In the 1970s, Senator Russell Long of Louisiana referred to welfare mothers as "brood mares." The slaveowners' control of fertility is mirrored again in the present economy which wants Black women's reproduction further reduced because Black workers and therefore Black children are increasingly seen as surplus. Norplant contraceptive implants, which can cause bleeding and other side effects, have become a eugenics weapon for judges and politicians.

Imagine labeling married-couple families as pathological breeding grounds of patriarchal domestic violence.

The myth of an intergenerational matriarchy of "welfare queens" is particularly disgusting since Black women were enslaved workers for over two centuries and have always had a high labor force participation rate and a disproportionate share of low wages and poverty. In 1900, Black women's labor force participation rate was 40.7 percent, white women's 16 percent. The 1960 rates were 42.2 percent for Black women and 33.6 percent for whites; in 1970, 49.5 percent and 42.6 percent; in 1980, 53.2 percent and 51.2 percent; and in 1991 they converged at 57 percent.

Rosemary Bray, a former editor of the *New York Times Book Review*, wrote a moving account of her own experience as an African-American child on welfare beginning in 1960 (*New York Times Magazine*, November 8, 1992). "What fueled our dreams and fired our belief that our lives could change for the better was the promise of the civil rights movement and the war on poverty," she recalls. "Had I been born a few years earlier, or a decade later, I might now be living on welfare in the Robert Taylor Homes or working as a hospital nurse's aide for $6.67 an hour." The demonization of the welfare mother allows "for denial about the depth and intransigence of racism" and reinforcement of the patriarchal notion "that women and children without a man are fundamentally damaged goods."

Bray cites a study of single mothers (low-wage workers and welfare recipients) by Rutgers University Professor Kathryn Edin, which demonstrates that "women, particularly unskilled women with children, get the worst jobs available, with the least amount of health care, and are the most frequently laid off." Bray observes, "the writers and scholars and politicians who wax most rhapsodic about the need to replace welfare with work make their harsh judgments from the comfortable and supportive environs of offices and libraries and think tanks. If they need to go to the bathroom midsentence, there is no one timing their absence. If they take longer than a half-hour for lunch, there is no one waiting to dock their pay. If their baby sitter gets sick, there is no risk of someone having taken their place at work by the next morning. Yet these are conditions that low-wage women routinely face, which inevitably lead to the cyclical nature of their welfare histories."

Poverty and AFDC

In 1990, there were about 3.4 million women, 374,000 men, and 7.7 million children under 18 receiving AFDC. The number of AFDC child recipients as a percent of children in poverty fell from 80.5 percent in 1973 to 59.9 percent in 1990. About 38 percent of AFDC families are white, 40 percent are Black, 17 percent are Latino, 3 percent are Asian, and 1 percent are Native American. There are disproportionately more people of color on welfare because disproportionately more people of color are poor and, as discussed below, they have disproportionately less access to other government benefits such as Social Security and Unemployment Insurance.

Contrary to image, most daughters in families who received welfare do not become welfare recipients as adults. And, women receiving welfare don't have more children than others. Most families on AFDC have one child (42 percent) or two children (30 percent); only 10 percent have more than three children.

Abramovitz notes in *Regulating the Lives of Women*, "the percentage of children in female-headed households has risen steadily since 1959, but the percentage of children receiving AFDC has remained constant at about 12 percent. Among black children, the divergence is even greater. Between 1972 and 1980, the number of black children living with just their mothers rose 20 percent while the number of black children receiving AFDC fell by 5 percent." Since 1970, the birth rates of unmarried Black women have fallen—while the birth rates of unmarried white women have risen—but the proportion of Black children born to unmarried mothers is growing because the birth rates of married Black women have fallen much more. (Some unmarried women, of course, are not single parents because they are raising children with male or female partners.)

The welfare system minimizes help and maximizes humiliation. When Barbara Sobel, head of the New York City Human Resources administration, posed as a welfare applicant to experience the system firsthand, she was misdirected, mistreated, and so "depersonalized," she says,

"I ceased to be." She remained on welfare, with a mandatory part-time job as a clerk in a city office, despite repeated pleas for full-time work, and learned that most recipients desperately want work (*New York Times*, February 5, 1993).

AFDC benefits have been chopped repeatedly as if, once you have too little money, it doesn't matter how little you have. Since 1972, inflation-adjusted AFDC benefits have plummeted 43 percent. The average monthly benefit for a family of three in 1991 was $367, which at $4,404 a year, is much less than half the official poverty threshold for a family of three that year, $10,973. And the official poverty threshold completely underestimates what it actually costs to feed, house, clothe, etc. Today just two necessities, food and especially housing, take 85 percent of a typical poor family's budget. Less than one out of four AFDC families live in public housing or receive any rent subsidies.

Below-subsistence welfare payments are governmental child abuse. The child-abusing budget cutters hide behind budget deficits (in 1991, AFDC accounted for less than 1 percent of federal outlays and states spent 2.2 percent of their revenues on AFDC) and their stereotypes of cheating "welfare queens." When California reduced its monthly AFDC payment for a mother and two children in 1991 from $694 (which was $2,645 below the annual poverty line) to $663, Governor Pete Wilson said it meant "one less six-pack per week." (*Equal Means*, Spring 1992)

Women turn to AFDC to support them and their children after divorce (when their incomes plummet because of no or low wages and no or low child support), after losing a job, after childbirth outside marriage, or while completing their education or job training. While most families receiving AFDC do so for two years or less, a minority of families become long-term recipients. As the 1992 House Committee on Ways and Means *Green Book* noted, "the typical recipient is a short-term user."

Aggressive, assertive women are penalized—they are abandoned by their men, end up impoverished, and are stigmatized as being unfeminine.

Long-term recipients have greater obstacles to getting off welfare such as lacking prior work experience, a high school degree or child care, or having poor health. Many women leave welfare—though often not poverty—after finding jobs and/or marrying men. Black women have a harder time doing either than white women, not because of a self-perpetuating "cycle of dependency," but a cycle of discrimination and demographics. It's fashionable to point to a "dearth of marriageable Black men," e.g., employed men earning above-poverty wages, without mentioning the dearth of Black men, period, as racism-fueled mortality takes its toll. The Black female-male ratio between the ages of 25 and 44, for example, was 100 to 87 in 1989, while it was 100 to 101 for whites.

Being married is neither necessary nor sufficient to avoid poverty. The 1991 poverty rates for married-couple families with children were 7.7 percent for whites, 14.3 percent for Blacks, and 23.5 percent for Latinos.

A new wave of policies is being enacted to address the "behavioral roots of poverty" and reinforce an old patriarchy with a "new paternalism." They punish unmarried women who have additional children—and punish those children—by denying women any increased benefits for new dependents and they reward women who marry. In the 1960s, the federal courts outlawed states' efforts to deny welfare benefits to "illegitimate" children and ended "midnight raids" to kick women off the rolls for having relationships with men. It remains to be seen how much the courts have changed as poor women and their legal advocates fight back.

Although two-thirds of AFDC recipients are children, critics make it sound like most recipients should be employed (then again, child labor is on the rise). Many women work or seek work outside the home while receiving welfare in spite of the near dollar-for-dollar reductions in benefits for wages and insufficient allowance for child care and other work expenses. In recent years, state and federal policy has imposed mandatory work and training programs. In 1990, nearly two-thirds of adult recipients were exempt from registration in work programs, most commonly because they had very young children to care for. Nearly 40 percent of AFDC families had at least one child two years old or younger. In a discriminatory, dangerous move to expand day care for AFDC recipients many states are exempting child care providers from health and safety regulations or loosening them. And prevailing "workfare" programs by whatever name do not help women transcend the growing ranks of the working poor.

Whose "culture of poverty"?

The myth of a "culture of poverty" masks the reality of an economy of impoverishment. A lot of single mother families are broke, but they aren't broken.

In 1991, 47.1 percent of all female-headed families with children under 18 were below the official poverty line as were 19.6 percent of male-headed families with children and no wives present. The respective rates were 39.6 and 16.5 percent for whites, 60.5 and 31.7 percent for Blacks, and 60.1 and 29.4 percent for Latinos. In other words, single father families have very high rates of poverty, but single mother families have even higher rates.

It's not surprising that many single parent households are poor since the U.S. government neither assures affordable child care nor provides the universal child supports common in Western Europe. France, Britain, Denmark, and Sweden, for example, have similar or higher proportions of births to unmarried women without U.S. proportions of poverty.

It shouldn't be surprising that Black and Latino single parent families have higher rates of poverty than white families since the earnings and job opportunities of people of color reflect continued educational and employment discrimination. The overall poverty rates of Black (28.5 percent) and Latino (26.2 percent) males are much closer to the poverty rate of all female-headed households with and without children, of any race (35.6 percent), than of white males (9.8 percent). And, it shouldn't be surprising that single mother families are the poorest of all since women are the lowest paid and women of color are doubly discriminated against. The fact that many female-headed households are poorer because women earn less than men is taken as a given in much welfare reform discussion, as if pay equity was a pipe dream not even worth mentioning.

A 1977 Department of Labor study found that if working women were paid what similarly qualified men earn, the number of poor families would decrease by half. In 1977, women working year-round, full-time earned 59 cents for every dollar earned by men. In 1991, they earned 70 cents. In 1991, the inflation-adjusted median income for full-time, year-round workers was $16,244 for Latina woman; $18,720 for Black women; $19,771 for Latino men; $20,794 for white women; $22,075 for Black men; and $30,266 for white men. Half the full-time workers in those categories made less than those amounts.

Two out of three workers who earn the minimum wage are women. Full-time work at minimum wage ($4.25 an hour) [the minimum wage will rise to $5.15 an hour in 1997] earns below the poverty line for a family of two. Discrimination is pervasive from the bottom to the top of the payscale and it's not because women are on the "mommy track." *Fortune* magazine (September 21, 1992) reports "that at the same level of management, the typical woman's pay is lower than her male colleague's— even when she has the exact same qualifications, works just as many years, relocates just as often, provides the main financial support for her family, takes no time off for personal reasons, and wins the same number of promotions to comparable jobs."

Nearly two out of three women with children under age six work outside the home. Most working mothers work full-time. Cutting child care is one of the ways states have balanced the budget on the backs of children and low-income families. According to a 1992 child care study commissioned by the Boston Foundation, after food, housing and taxes, child care is the biggest expense for working parents of all incomes. Boston's child care costs are among the nation's highest. In a 1988 survey of Boston-area employees, families reported spending an average of $130 a week for child care (nationally that year child care teaching staff, mostly women, had average earnings of only $9,363, while sanitation workers earned $19,163 and workers in cigarette factories earned $30,590). Because of decreased state-funded child care subsidies, only one-third of the 10,000 Boston children eligible for such subsidies will find them.

Under the upperclass

Terms like "underclass" and "persistent poverty" imply that poverty persists in spite of society's commitment to eliminate it. In reality, the socioeconomic system reproduces poverty no matter how persistently people are trying to get out or stay out of poverty.

As Adolph Reed Jr. writes in *Radical America* (January 1992) in a critique of various underclass theories, "behavioral tendencies supposedly characterizing the underclass exist generally throughout the society. Drug use, divorce, educational underattainment, laziness, and empty consumerism exist no less in upper status suburbs than in inner-city bantustans. The difference lies not in the behavior but in the social position of those exhibiting it" and in their access to safety nets. And in their imprisonment rates.

A 1990 study in the *New England Journal of Medicine* found that substance abuse rates are slightly higher for white women than nonwhite women, but nonwhite women are ten times more likely to be reported to authorities. And, while mothers are increasingly prosecuted for drug use during pregnancy, the doors of most drug treatment centers remain closed to pregnant women. Similarly, Black kids are less likely to use drugs than white kids (according to government studies), but much more likely to be stigmatized and jailed for it. If the irrational drug laws were applied equally, we'd see a lot more handcuffed white movie stars, rich teenagers, politicians, doctors, stockbrokers, and CIA officers on the TV news, trying to hide their faces.

The stereotype "welfare queen" lazily collects government checks and reproduces poverty by passing on her pathologies to her many children.

Low-income people and communities, like middle- and upper-class people and communities, have a mix of strengths and weaknesses, needs and capacities. But poor communities are uniquely portrayed as the negative sum of their needs and "risks." All people and communities need services. In higher-income communities, people needing doctors or psychologists, lawyers or drug treatment, birth control or abortion, tutors or child care, can afford pricey private practitioners and avoid the stigma that often accompanies stingy public social services. In lower-income communities they cannot. This problem is especially bad in the United States because it lags far behind all other industrialized democracies in assuring the basic human needs of its people.

When health care is a privilege, not a right, children die. But it's cheaper to blame their mothers than provide real universal health care (not Clinton's "managed competition"). Seventy countries provide prenatal care to *all* pregnant women and many have policies requiring *paid* maternity leave. The United States does not. An Ohio study found that a woman on pregnancy leave is 10 times more likely to lose her job than one on medical leave for other reasons (*New York Times*, January 12, 1993). More children die before their first birthday in the United States per capita than in 21 other countries. Nationally, the infant mortality rate for Black babies is more than twice as high as for whites—the widest gap since 1940, when race specific data were first collected. In Boston, it is three times higher.

The *Boston Globe* (September 10, 1990) investigated "birth in the 'death zones'," illuminating the link between racism, poverty, inadequate health care, and infant mortality. A later *Globe* editorial contrasted the response to that article with reaction to news that a dolphin was going to be dispatched from Boston's aquarium to the U.S. Navy: "Urgent appeals to save the dolphin are pouring in. The dolphin's innocence and dependency upon human kindness are noted. Money is no object to assuring it tender, loving care." For "the babies, most of them black and Hispanic," the common reaction was it's their mothers' fault and the babies deserve what they get. The majority of letters and phone calls concerning the babies, the *Globe* noted, "are ugly and racist. The mothers are termed 'moral-less' and 'irresponsible pigs.' The babies are described as 'inferior' and 'leeches.' They are degraded as 'trash that begets trash'."

One out of four children is born into poverty in the United States—the highest official rate of any industrialized nation. The official 1991 child poverty rate was 21.8 percent (25.5 percent for children under age three). For white children, it was 16.8 percent; for Latino children, 40.4 percent; and for Black children, 45.9 percent. Poverty rates would be even higher if they counted families whose incomes fell below the poverty line after taxes, and if the poverty threshold was adjusted upward to reflect, not just an inflation-multiplied out of date standard, but the real cost of living. The last time the Department of Labor compiled a "lower family budget," in 1981, it was 65 percent above that year's official poverty line for the same size family. In their book on the working poor, *The Forgotten Americans*, John Schwarz and Thomas Volgy show that based on a stringent economy budget a family of four in 1990 needed an income of about $20,700, or 155 percent of the 1990 official poverty line of $13,360.

Many countries provide a children's allowance or other universal public benefit for families raising children. The United States does not. Throughout the 1980s, the U.S. government preached family values without valuing families. "Under our tax laws," Colorado Congresswoman Pat Schroeder was quoted in a *Time* feature on children (October 8, 1990), "the deduction for a Thoroughbred horse is greater than that for children."

The income gap

Everything from prenatal care to college is rationed by money in a country where income inequality has grown so much that the top 4 percent of Americans earned as much in wages and salaries in 1989 as the bottom 51 percent; in 1959, the top 4 percent earned as much as the bottom 35 percent. The average chief executive officer (CEO) of a large corporation earned as much in salary as 42 factory workers in 1980 and 104 factory workers in 1991 (Japan's CEOs earn about as much as 18 factory workers).

The top 1 percent of families now have a net worth much greater than that of the bottom 90 percent. In 1989, reports the Economic Policy Institute, the top 1 percent of families had 37.7 percent of total net worth (assets minus debt) and the bottom 90 percent had 29.2 percent; the bottom 95 percent had 40.7 percent. The top fifth of families had 83.6 percent of net worth; the upper middle fifth, 12.3 percent; the middle fifth, 4.9 percent; the lower middle fifth, 0.8 percent; and the bottom fifth, –1.7 percent. Looking at family income, the top fifth (families with pretax incomes of $61,490 and above in 1990) had 55.5 percent; the upper middle fifth, 20.7 percent; the middle fifth, 13.3 percent; the lower middle fifth, 7.6 percent; and the bottom fifth, 3.1 percent.

U.S. wealth concentration is now more extreme than any time since 1929, and getting worse. For many Americans there's an endless economic depression. The shrinking middle class is misled into thinking those below them on the economic ladder are pulling them down, when in reality those at the top of the ladder are pushing everyone down.

The stereotype of deadbeat poor people masks the growing reality of dead-end jobs. It is fashionable to point to the so-called breakdown of the family as a cause of poverty and ignore the breakdown in wages. The average inflation-adjusted earnings of nonsupervisory workers crashed 19 percent between 1973 and 1990. Minimum wage is 23 percent below its average value during the 1970s. For more and more Americans and their children, work is not a ticket out of poverty, but a condition of poverty.

Living standards are falling for younger generations, despite the fact that many households have two wage earners. The inflation-adjusted median income for families with children headed by persons younger than 30 plummeted 32 percent between 1973 and 1990. Forty percent of all children in families headed by someone younger than 30 were living in poverty in 1990—including one out of four children in white young families.

Although two-thirds of AFDC recipients are children, critics make it sound like most recipients should be employed.

The entry-level wage for high school graduates fell 22 percent between 1979 and 1991, a reflection, reports the Economic Policy Institute, of "the shift toward lower-paying industries, the lower value of the minimum wage, less unionization" and other trends. Entry level wages for college graduates fell slightly overall (–0.2 percent) between 1979 and 1991, but Black college graduates lost over 3 percent and Latino college graduates lost nearly 15 percent. Between 1979 and 1990, the proportion of full-time, year-round workers, ages 18 to 24, paid low wages (below $12,195 in 1990) jumped from 23 percent in 1979 to over 43 percent in 1990. Among young women workers, the figure is nearly one in two workers. And low-wage jobs are often dead-end jobs with low or no benefits (e.g. health insurance, paid vacation, pension), round-the-clock shifts, and little prospect of advancement.

During the 1960s and 1970s, Blacks were about twice as likely to be unemployed as whites, according to official, undercounting statistics. In the 1980s, the gap widened: when white unemployment was 8.4 percent in 1983, Black unemployment was 19.5 percent. When white unemployment was 4.1 percent in 1990, Black unemployment was 2.76 times higher at 11.3 percent. Black college graduates had a jobless rate 2.24 times that of white college graduates. As the Urban Institute documented in a 1990 study using carefully matched and trained pairs of white and Black young men applying for entry-level jobs, discrimination against Black job seekers, is "entrenched and widespread."

To make matters worse, most unemployed people do not receive unemployment insurance benefits. An average one-third of the officially counted unemployed nationwide received benefits from 1984 to 1989; the figure rose to 42 percent in the severe recession year of 1991 (76 percent received benefits during the 1975 recession). Eligibility varies by state and unemployment insurance typically lasts only a maximum of 26 weeks whether or not you've found a job.

Low wage workers, disproportionately women and people of color, are less likely than other workers to qualify for unemployment benefits (they may not earn enough or meet work history requirements) and, when they do qualify, their unemployment payments are only a portion of their meager wages. When the New Deal–era Unemployment Insurance and Social Security programs were established, the occupations excluded from coverage—such as private domestic workers, agricultural laborers, government and nonprofit employees—were ones with large numbers of women and people of color. A recent General Accounting Office study reported in the *New York Times* (May 11, 1992) found that after accounting for such factors as age, education, and types of disability, "blacks with serious ailments have been much more likely than whites to be rejected for benefits" under the Social Security Disability Insurance and Supplemental Security Income programs.

Unlike many other countries, U.S. Social Security penalizes women for work force absences due to pregnancy or care of children and, until 1976, pregnant women could be denied unemployment benefits. Domestic workers became entitled to Social Security pensions in 1951, but received virtually no Unemployment Insurance protection until 1978, when federal law required coverage of certain farm workers, most state and local government employees, and some private, household workers. Workers forced to leave their jobs to care for newborns or ill family members have been denied unemployment benefits because they are "voluntarily" unemployed.

"Recent studies in several states have found that a substantial proportion of new AFDC families are headed by individuals who have recently lost their jobs," reports the Center on Budget and Policy Priorities. "For unemployed people who do not have children, little or no cash assistance may be available if they fail to receive unemployment benefits. Many states and localities lack any general assistance program or else limit such a program to people who are elderly or have disabilities."

In the unusually blunt words of *Time* magazine (September 28, 1992), "Official statistics fail to reveal the extent of the pain. Unemployment stands at 7.6 percent . . . but more people are experiencing distress. A comprehensive tally would include workers who are employed well below their skill level, those who cannot find more than a part-time job, people earning poverty-level wages, workers who have been jobless for more than four weeks at a time and all those who have grown discouraged and quit looking. Last year those distressed workers totaled 36 million, or 40 percent of the American labor force, according to the Washington-based Economic Policy Institute."

"We never meant to quit our jobs. They quit on us," says a former Rath Meatpacking employee from Waterloo, Iowa, quoted by Jacqueline Jones in *The Dispossessed*. Corporations are permanently downsizing their workforces and shifting more operations (including service sector jobs such as data processing) to countries where workers have even lower wages and few or no rights. The newer U.S. jobs not only pay less than disappearing unionized jobs, but employers are replacing full-time workers with part-time and temporary workers with even lower benefits and job security.

Broken ladders

Education is often portrayed as the great ladder out of poverty. But four decades after *Brown v. Board of Education* many schools are separate and unequal by race and economic status. Public school budgets are heavily determined by private property taxes. In Massachusetts in 1991, the federal share of school funding was 4.9 percent, the state share 37.1 percent, and the local share 58 percent. "Typically," writes Jonathan Kozol in *Savage Inequalities*, "very poor communities place high priority on education, and they often tax themselves at higher rates than do the very affluent communities," but the higher rates cannot offset the income gaps. And, like the mortgage interest deduction, the property tax deduction on federal taxes subsidizes higher income people the most.

The wide variations in local school funding mean that wealthier districts spend two to four times as much per pupil than poorer ones, making the education system more reflective of apartheid than democracy. Wealthier citizens argue that lack of money isn't the problem in poorer schools—family values are—until proposals are made to make school spending more even. Then money matters for those who already have more.

Single mother families are the poorest of all since women are the lowest paid and women of color are doubly discriminated against.

Despite continued discriminatory school resources and expectations, the percentage of Blacks (ages 25–29), who are high school graduates or more has steadily climbed from 22.3 percent in 1947 to 76.6 percent in 1980 to 81.7 percent in 1991, while whites went from 54.9 percent in 1947 to 86.9 percent in 1980 to 85.8 percent in 1991. The percentage of Blacks with four or more years of college has risen from 2.8 percent in 1947 to 11.6 percent in 1980 to 13.4 percent in 1990, while whites went from 5.9 percent in 1947 to 23.7 percent in 1980 and 24.2 percent in 1990. The percentage of Blacks with college degrees fell to 11 percent in 1991, as skyrocketing tuition (rising faster than health care and housing) and educational cutbacks took their toll at a time when a college degree is increasingly crucial for decent pay. Blacks and Latinos are shortchanged in pay at all levels of educational attainment and routinely steered into lower wage fields.

The cycle of unequal opportunity has been reinforced by tax reform favoring the wealthy and ballooning the national debt. In 1968, the United States had a progressive personal income tax with a bottom tax rate of 14 percent and a top rate of 75 percent. Now—after the tax cuts advertised to stimulate investment, jobs, and trickle-down wealth—it has three rates: 15, 28, and 31 percent. State and local sales, excise, and property taxes are highly regressive (the poor pay a greater portion of their income than the rich). So is the Social Security payroll tax, which increased 30 percent between 1978 and 1990 and exempts incomes above a cap ($53,400 as of 1991), though even the wealthiest receive Social Security. Making things still worse, state and local governments are rushing to expand lotteries, video poker, and other government-promoted gambling to raise revenues, disproportionately from the poor, which they should be raising from a fair tax system.

In *Putting People First*, Bill Clinton and Al Gore offer a mix of coded and partial policies to address poverty: "To ensure that no one with a family who works full-time has to raise children in poverty, we will increase the Earned Income Tax Credit to make up the difference between a family's earnings and the poverty level." At the same time, they recommend, "Scrap the current welfare system to make welfare a second chance, not a way of life. We will empower people on welfare with the education, retraining, and child care they need for up to two years so they can break the cycle of dependency. After that, those who are able will be required to work, either in the private sector or through community service." President Clinton asserted to the nation's governors in February 1993, "we will remove the incentive for staying in poverty," people should not "draw a check for doing nothing when they can do something." So far, Clinton has backpedaled fast on plans to cut unemployment and underemployment and assure that college is not an unaffordable privilege.

Welfare reform and other ideas are discussed more fully in *Mandate for Change*, the Progressive Policy Institute/Democratic Leadership Council blueprint for Clinton. It's revealing that in the chapter "Replacing Welfare with Work," the only race repeatedly mentioned is Black and the only age given is the atypical "15-year-old welfare mother with a new baby." The chapter is written as if being poor, Black, being on welfare, and being innercity "underclass" are all synonymous.

As Marion Wright Edelman, president of the Children's Defense Fund (the organization chaired formerly by Hillary Clinton and Donna Shalala) told the Clinton Economic Summit, "Contrary to popular myth, the majority of poor children are not black, not on welfare and don't live in inner cities, but live in working families and outside inner cities in small town, rural and suburban America. Between 1989 and 1992, nearly one-quarter of the 1.7 million children who fell into poverty lived in two-parent white families, many of whom thought they'd never be out of work, need food stamps or face homelessness or hunger. New Hampshire reported the highest rate of growth in food stamp participation in the nation over the past three years."

It is fashionable to point to the so-called breakdown of the family as a cause of poverty and ignore the breakdown in wages.

In the words of the Children's Defense Fund, "The slow, grinding violence of poverty takes an American child's life every 53 minutes. The deadly, quick violence of guns takes an American child's life every three hours." Single mothers do not direct the economy—legal or underground. They don't direct the drug war, the National Rifle Association, the military, or the television and movie industries which teach children violence through entertainment and government action.

Pointing fingers at an "underclass culture of poverty" diverts attention and anger from the poverty-reproducing upperclass culture of greed. While subsidizing the luxury lifestyle of corporate kingpins and bailing out wealthy bank speculators, politicians pretend that below-subsistence subsidies for poor women and children are destroying the family and bringing down the American economy. Upperclass white America has been built on centuries of discriminatory subsidy and violence, from slavery to segregated suburbanization, Indian removal to "urban renewal," redbaiting, redlining, and union-busting. It's way past time to break upperclass dependency on the cycle of unequal opportunity.

Selected Data Resources

U.S. Bureau of the Census, *Statistical Abstract of the United States 1992; Poverty in the United States: 1991; Money Income of Households, Families, and Persons in the United States: 1991; Workers with Low Earnings: 1964 to 1990.*

U.S. Department of Health and Human Services, *Characteristics and Financial Circumstances of AFDC Recipients: Fiscal Year 1990.*

U.S. House of Representatives, Committee on Ways and Means, *1992 Green Book: Overview of Entitlement Programs*, May 15 1992; *Background Material on Family Income and Benefit Changes*, December 19, 1991.

10

Single Motherhood
Is a Legitimate Choice

Katha Pollitt

Katha Pollitt is an associate editor of the Nation, *a liberal journal of opinion.*

The decision to become a single mother is a rational choice for women who want children but do not need the economic security that marriage has traditionally provided. Society should recognize the legitimacy of this choice rather than blaming single mothers for social breakdown.

Murphy Brown's baby apparently has a lot of real-life company. According to a census-bureau report, the percentages of white women and women with some college education who have become mothers without marrying more than doubled between 1983 and 1993, to 14.6 percent and 11.3 percent, respectively; among women with professional or managerial jobs, the figure has almost tripled, to 8.3 percent. While the numbers are small—most unwed mothers are poor and thus disproportionately black or Hispanic—they show that single motherhood cannot be explained away by words like *inner city*, *welfare dependency* and *pathology*.

The usual suspects

Nonetheless, if you listen closely you can hear the hum of word processors as family-values advocates labor through the night, turning out articles and speeches bemoaning the new statistics and rounding up the usual suspects: feminism, promiscuity, the media, the sixties.

What if, instead of trying to bully women to the altar, we ask why they're no longer running up the aisles? Women have often been warned that they can't have a career, a husband *and* a child; they have to pick two out of three. It's assumed that for middle-class women, the contest is between the career and the kid. As it turns out, many women have a different set of priorities. Could it be that they're on to something?

Maybe marriage no longer serves women very well. Historically, lucky

Katha Pollitt, "Motherhood Without Marriage," *Glamour*, October 1993. Reprinted by permission of the author.

women married for love and still do—I'm sure that most of today's un-wed employed moms would be pleased to tie the knot with a diaper-changing Mr. Right—but beneath the hearts and flowers, middle-class marriage was an economic bargain. He supported her; she minded the house and children.

Marriage was the only path

With rare exceptions, marriage was the only path to female adulthood: a home of one's own, community standing, a sex life, children. Barred from professional training and good jobs, threatened with disgrace and the loss of her baby if she got pregnant, mocked as a spinster if she stayed unwed past her early twenties, a woman was pushed into marriage by just about every social institution: family, religion, neighbors, custom, law, school, the workplace, doctors of soul and body.

None of this is true today. If women can support themselves, they don't need to marry for what was politely called security but was, to put it bluntly, money. If single women can have sex, their own homes, the respect of friends and interesting work, they don't need to tell themselves that any marriage is better than none. Why not have a child on one's own? Children are a joy; many men are not. To take care of a child makes sense: Children cannot cook their own meals, make their own doctor's appointments, do their own laundry. To take care of a husband after working all day makes much less sense, but most men still seem to expect it. All around them, single women see divorced women raising kids, of-ten with little or no child support, and hear married moms say they might as well be single for all the help they get from their mates. If sin-gle women increasingly see marriage and motherhood as separate com-mitments, perhaps the reason is that they are.

Maybe marriage no longer serves women very well.

The collapse of the traditional middle-class marriage bargain has left both sexes bewildered and is a major cause of the much-discussed open hostility between men and women. But how can you make the sexes act as if they needed each other to survive when they don't? All they need each other for is love, and love is hard to find. That is the nettle the family-values proponents refuse to grasp. They keep talking as if women can be corralled into marriage by appeals to morality and self-sacrifice or punitive social policies. But the futility of their cause is shown by the fee-ble measures they propose: deglamorizing single motherhood, emphasiz-ing fatherhood, stigmatizing single moms or their kids.

Comparisons

Critics of single motherhood cite studies showing higher rates of every-thing from crime to bad grades in single mothers' children. What they don't tell you is that most of this results from the crushing poverty in which so many single mothers live. Among middle-class kids, the only fair comparison is between those raised by a single mother and those raised by unhappily married parents. A bad marriage may be the only alternative that a single mother faces. Here, too, the difference to the children vanishes.

There isn't any way, in our modern, secular society, to reconnect marriage and maternity. These days, parents aren't interested in banishing unmarried pregnant daughters; they're more likely to be thrilled to be grandparents. We'd have to bring back the whole nineteenth century: restore the cult of virginity and the double standard, ban birth control, restrict divorce, kick women out of decent jobs, force unwed pregnant women to put their babies up for adoption on pain of social death, make out-of-wedlock children legal nonpersons.

If women can support themselves, they don't need to marry for what was politely called security but was, to put it bluntly, money.

None of this will happen, so why not come to terms with reality? We can't put the genie of women's economic, sexual and social independence back into the bottle of marriage, because marriage, at bottom, is based on the absence of those things. Instead of trying to make women—and men—adapt to an outworn institution, we should adapt our institutions to the lives people actually live. Single mothers need paid parental leave, day care, flexible schedules, child support, pediatricians with evening hours and schools that recognize that mothers have jobs. Most of all, they need equal pay and comparable worth. What they don't need is sermons.

Organizations to Contact

The editors have compiled the following list of organizations concerned with the issues debated in this book. The descriptions are derived from materials provided by the organizations themselves. All have publications or information available for interested readers. The list was compiled on the date of publication of the present volume; names, addresses, phone and fax numbers, and e-mail/internet addresses may change. Be aware that many organizations take several weeks or longer to respond to inquiries, so allow as much time as possible.

Center for Research on Women
Wellesley College
106 Central St.
Wellesley, MA 02181-8259
(617) 283-2500
fax: (617) 283-2504
internet: http://www.wellesley.edu/WCW/CRW/crwhome.html

The center is a community of scholars engaged in research, programs, and publications that examine the lives of women, men, and children in a changing world. Its research is used to shape public policy and promote positive social and institutional change concerning the way society views women. Among the center's numerous publications are the biannual *Research Report* and the papers "Welfare Reform: Causes and Contradictions," "The Work and Family Responsibilities of Black Women Single Parents," and "Back to Basics: Women's Poverty and Welfare Reform."

Children's Defense Fund
25 E St. NW
Washington, DC 20001
(202) 628-8787
fax: (202) 662-3510

The fund provides long-range advocacy on behalf of the nation's children and teenagers. It works with individuals and groups to change policies and practices resulting in the neglect or maltreatment of millions of children. The fund publishes the monthly newsletter *CDF Reports*, the research paper "Enforcing Child Support: Are States Doing the Job?" and the books *A Black Community Crusade and Covenant for Protecting Children* and *Wasting America's Future: The Children's Defense Fund's Report on the Costs of Child Poverty.*

Concerned Women for America (CWA)
370 L'Enfant Promenade SW, Suite 800
Washington, DC 20024
(202) 488-7000
fax: (202) 488-0806

CWA is an educational and legal defense foundation that seeks to protect the rights of the family and preserve traditional American values. It publishes *Family Voice* eleven times a year, which periodically addresses the importance of the traditional family through articles such as "Making Room for Daddy."

Families International
11700 W. Lake Park Dr.
Milwaukee, WI 53224
(414) 359-1040
fax: (414) 359-1074

Families International is a nonprofit publisher established in association with Family Service America, Family Foundation of North America, and Family Enterprises. Its primary subsidiary, Family Service America, is dedicated to strengthening family life through services, education, and advocacy. Families International publishes the scholarly journal *Families in Society: The Journal of Contemporary Human Services*, which periodically includes articles on single-parent families, as well as the video *Single Parenting*.

Institute for American Values
1841 Broadway, Suite 211
New York, NY 10023
(212) 246-3942
fax: (212) 541-6665

The institute is a research organization that focuses on issues affecting the well-being of families and children in the United States. It publishes the papers "Beyond the Murphy Brown Debate: Ideas for Family Policy," "Marriage, Parenting, and Women's Quest for Equality," and "The Family Values of Americans" and the books *Fatherless America* and *Life Without Father*.

Men's Defense Association
17854 Lyons St.
Forest Lake, MN 55025
(612) 464-7887
fax: (612) 464-7135
e-mail: mensdefens@aol.com

The association is composed of male victims of both actual and potential sex discrimination. Its members hope to obtain equal rights under the law for all males and to promote and engage in activities that will strengthen the marriage relationship and family life. It publishes the newsletter the *Liberator* and a variety of papers, including "Don't Blame Me, Daddy," "The Garbage Generation," and "Divorce: What Everyone Should Know to Beat the Racket."

Mothers At Home (MAH)
8310A Old Courthouse Rd.
Vienna, VA 22182
(703) 827-5903
fax: (703) 790-8587

MAH is the largest national organization supporting mothers who choose to stay at home and raise their families. It works to affirm a mother's choice to be at home and serves as an advocate for children's need for generous amounts of their parents' time. The organization seeks to ensure that public debate appropriately considers issues of importance to mothers today. MAH publishes the books *Discovering Motherhood* and *What's a Smart Woman like You Doing at Home?* and the monthly journal *Welcome Home.*

National Council for Single Adoptive Parents
PO Box 15084
Chevy Chase, MD 20825
(202) 966-6367
fax: (202) 966-6367

The council is composed of single persons who have adopted or wish to adopt children. It informs public and private agencies of legislation and research applying to single-person adoption. The council publishes the quarterly *News for Single Adoptive Parents* and the *Handbook for Single Adoptive Parents.*

Single Mothers by Choice (SMC)
PO Box 1642
Gracie Square Station
New York, NY 10028
(212) 988-0993

SMC offers support and information for single women who are considering motherhood or who have chosen to become mothers. It presents the opportunity for women to network with others about the issues of single motherhood and provides a peer group for their children. SMC publishes a quarterly newsletter and the book *Single Mothers by Choice: A Guidebook for Single Women Who Are Considering or Have Chosen Motherhood.*

Single Parent Resource Center
31 E. 28th St., 2nd Fl.
New York, NY 10016
(212) 951-7030
fax: (212) 951-7037

The center, founded in 1975, is devoted exclusively to the preservation of single-parent families. It offers numerous programs developed to assist a wide range of single parents, including homeless parents, women returning to the community from prison, and low-income working parents. The center publishes "Working with Single Parents: A Guide for Group Developers" and the brochures *Ten Tips to Start a New Life* and *Tips for Working Parents.*

Bibliography

Books

Mary Frances Berry	*The Politics of Parenthood: Child Care, Women's Rights, and the Myth of the Good Mother.* New York: Viking, 1993.
David Blankenhorn	*Fatherless America: Confronting Our Most Urgent Social Problem.* New York: BasicBooks, 1995.
Bette J. Dickerson, ed.	*African American Single Mothers: Understanding Their Lives and Families.* Newbury Park, CA: Sage Publications, 1994.
Irwin Garfinkel, Sara S. McLanahan, and Philip K. Robins, eds.	*Child Support and Child Well-Being.* Washington, DC: Urban Institute Press, 1995.
Linda Gordon	*Pitied but Not Entitled: Single Mothers and the History of Welfare.* New York: Free Press, 1994.
Robert L. Griswold	*Fatherhood in America: A History.* New York: BasicBooks, 1993.
Penny Kaganoff and Susan Spano, eds.	*Women on Divorce: A Bedside Companion.* Orlando, FL: Harcourt Brace, 1995.
Elizabeth A. Mulroy	*The New Uprooted: Single Mothers in Urban Life.* Westport, CT: Greenwood Press, 1995.
Valerie Polakow	*Lives on the Edge: Single Mothers and Their Children in the Other America.* Chicago: University of Chicago Press, 1993.
David Popenoe	*Life Without Father: Compelling New Evidence That Fatherhood and Marriage are Indispensable for the Good of Children and Society.* New York: Free Press, 1996.
Richard Weissbourd	*The Vulnerable Child: What Really Hurts America's Children and What We Can Do About It.* Reading, MA: Addison-Wesley, 1996.

Periodicals

Addresses are provided for periodicals not indexed in the *Social Science Index*, the *Alternative Press Index*, the *Reader's Guide to Periodical Literature*, or the *Index to Legal Periodicals and Books*.

John Attarian	"Bad Fathering Breeds National Decline," *St. Croix Review*, October 1995. Available from PO Box 244, Stillwater, MN 55082-0244.
Michelle Brown-Glover with Betsy Krebs	"Making the System Work for Teen Mothers (and Their Children)," *Foster Care Youth United*, January/February 1996. Available from 144 W. 27th St., #8R, New York, NY 10001.

Robert P. Casey — "Saving the American Family," *World & I*, January 1996. Available from 3600 New York Ave. NE, Washington, DC 20002.

Richard Cohen — "Societal Transformation to Single-Parent Families," *Liberal Opinion Week*, July 26, 1993. Available from 108 E. Fifth St., Vinton, IA 52349.

Stephanie Coontz — "The Way We Weren't: The Myth and Reality of the 'Traditional' Family," *National Forum*, vol. 75, no. 3, Summer 1995. Available from Box 16000, Louisiana State University, Baton Rouge, LA 70893-1410.

Kenneth J. Cooper — "Black Fathers Do Pay Child Support," *Emerge*, October 1995. Available from One BET Plaza, 1900 W Pl. NE, Washington, DC 20018-1211.

Susan Crabtree — "Politics of Family Values," *Insight*, June 17, 1996. Available from 3600 New York Ave. NE, Washington, DC 20002.

Dan Davenport — "Why We Need Fathers," *Better Homes and Gardens*, June 1996.

Destiny Magazine — "Single Fathers: Can They Stem the Tide?" June 1995. Available from PO Box 1000, Selma, OR 97538.

Elena Duckett and Maryse H. Richards — "Maternal Employment and the Quality of Daily Experience for Young Adolescents of Single Mothers," *Journal of Family Psychology*, vol. 9, no. 4, 1995. Available from the American Psychological Association, 750 First St. NE, Washington, DC 20002-4242.

Lloyd Eby and Charles A. Donovan — "Single Parents and Damaged Children: The Fruits of the Sexual Revolution," *World & I*, July 1993.

David Elkind — "The Family in the Postmodern World," *National Forum*, vol. 75, no. 3, Summer 1995.

The Family in America: New Research — Entire issue on families, May 1995. Available from the Rockford Institute, 934 N. Main St., Rockford, IL 61103.

Don Feder — "Fatherless Families Fuel Crime Explosion," *Conservative Chronicle*, December 1, 1993. Available from 9 Second St. NW, Hampton, IA 50441.

William A. Galston — "Braking Divorce for the Sake of Children," *American Enterprise*, May/June 1996.

Rob Gurwitt — "The Politics of Divorce," *Governing*, May 1996.

D. Hollander — "Teenage Fathers May Play Larger Role in Child Care Than Is Often Thought," *Family Planning Perspectives*, March/April 1996. Available from Circulation Manager, 111 Fifth Ave., New York, NY 10003.

Barbara Jean Hope — "The Myths, and the Lies, About Unwed Motherhood," *People's Weekly World*, November 18, 1995. Available from 235 W. 23rd St., New York, NY 10011.

Michele Ingrassia — "Daughters of Murphy Brown: Family: The Most Rapid Rise in Single Motherhood Is Among Educated, Professional Women," *Newsweek*, August 2, 1993.

Michele Ingrassia   "Endangered Family," *Newsweek*, August 30, 1993.

Janine Jackson   "The 'Crisis' of Teen Pregnancy: Girls Pay the Price for
                         Media Distortion," *Extra!*, March/April 1994.

R. Cort Kirkwood   "No-Fault Divorces Under Increasing Attack," *Insight*,
                         June 17, 1996.

George Liebmann   "Back to the Maternity Home," *American Enterprise*,
                         January/February 1995.

Michael Lynch   "Mythical Murphy Brown," *Weekly Standard*, December
                         18, 1995. Available from PO Box 96153, Washington,
                         DC 20090-6153.

Sara S. McLanahan   "The Consequences of Single Motherhood," *American
                         Prospect*, Summer 1994. Available from PO Box 383080,
                         Cambridge, MA 02238-3080.

Charles Murray   "Does Welfare Bring More Babies?" *Public Interest*, Spring
                         1994.

Kim Phillips   "Taking the Heat Off Teen Moms," *In These Times*,
                         March 4, 1996.

David Popenoe   "The American Family Crisis," *National Forum*, vol. 75,
                         no. 3, Summer 1995.

Dan Quayle   "Restoring Basic Values: Strengthening the Family," *Vital
                         Speeches of the Day*, June 15, 1992.

Hanna Rosin   "Separation Anxiety," *New Republic*, May 6, 1996.

Carl Rowan   "Illegitimacy: Reflections of a Broad Moral Erosion," *Liberal
                         Opinion Week*, January 1, 1996.

David Segal   "Motherload: Should We Be Forcing Single Welfare
                         Moms to Work Full Time?" *Washington Monthly*, October
                         1992.

Judith Stacey   "The Family Values Fable," *National Forum*, vol. 75, no.
                         3, Summer 1995.

Judith Stacey   "The Smoke Screen of 'Family Values,'" *Insight*, November
                         29, 1993.

Glenn T. Stanton   "Twice As Strong," *Christian American*, March/April 1996.
                         Available from 1801-L Sara Dr., Chesapeake, VA 23320.

St. Croix Review   "The Failed Revolution: A Culture of Divorce," October
                         1995.

Richard Weissbourd   "Divided Families, Whole Children," *American Prospect*,
                         Summer 1994.

Cheryl Wetzstein   "The Fatherhood Deficit," *World & I*, November 1995.

Barbara Dafoe   "Divorce and Kids: The Evidence Is In," *Reader's Digest*,
Whitehead   July 1993.

Index

Abramovitz, Mimi, 83, 87
Achenbach, Thomas, 55, 56
Aid to Families with Dependent Children
  (AFDC), 85, 86
  benefits have plummeted, 88
  limitation of benefits, 80
  relationship to poverty, 86
All Our Kin (Stack), 23
American Prospect, 68
America's Children (Hernandez), 67
America's Smallest School: The Family
  (Barton), 29
Anderson, Elijah, 68
Atlantic Monthly, 64, 68
Auletta, Ken, 22

Backlash (Faludi), 84
Ballard, Charles, 61
Barton, Paul, 29
Bergen, Candice, 18
Black Feminist Thought (Collins), 84
Blankenhorn, David, 53
Block, Jack, 67
Boot Camp for New Dads, 61
Boston Foundation, 90
Boston Globe, 91
Boston's Immigrants (Handlin), 83
Boyz N the Hood, 83
Bradshaw, John, 18
Bray, Rosemary, 86, 87
Brown, Laurene Krasney, 20
Brown, Marc, 20
Brown v. Board of Education, 94
Burton, Linda, 68
Bush, George, 71

California Children of Divorce Study, 23, 26
Carnegie Council on Children, 21
Carter Administration, 12
Casey Foundation, 54
Chambers, David, 32
Cherlin, Andrew, 15, 28, 34, 67, 69
children
  connections with grandparents, 57–59
  and divorce
    effects of, 28–30, 44–48
      are exaggerated, 66
      parents underestimate, 43
    stresses from, 45
    threatens bond with father, 27–28
    views on, 42–44
  economic hardship linked to problems
    of, 68–69
  increase in poverty among
    family disruption is cause of, 34
    social factors cause, 80–81, 88, 92
  parental investment in
    is undermined by regime effect, 39–40
    of widows, outcomes of, 38

Children's Defense Fund, 96
child support, 25
Christian Century, 55
classism
  is behind condemnation of poor women,
    76
Clinton, Bill, 62, 78, 96
Cohen, Susan, 48
Collins, Patricia Hill, 84, 85
Conroy, Pat, 26
conservative right
  equates family values with nuclear
    family, 63
Coontz, Stephanie, 19, 74, 75, 83
Cortez, Ernesto, Jr., 57
*Creative Divorce: A New Opportunity for
  Personal Growth*, 22
crime
  family disruption as cause of, 34–36
  increases due to single parenthood, 49
Cuomo, Mario, 50

Daly, Martin, 31
*Dinosaurs Divorce: A Guide for Changing
  Families* (Brown and Brown), 20, 21
Dionne, E.J., 70
discrimination
  against nonwhites in employment, 89–90
  against single mothers, 74–75
Dise-Lewis, Jeanne, 42
Dispossessed, The (Jones), 94
divorce
  boom in, 41
  causes economic hardship, 54–55
  as chain of events, 26–27, 66
  effects on children, 28–30, 44–48, 73
    behavioral changes, 45–48
    gender differences, 46–47
  living standards after
    gender differences, 25
  rates of, 15
  social sanctions against, 14
    conservative right would restore, 63
  stress on children of, 45
  violent conflicts not major cause of, 43
Divorce and New Beginnings, 19

Earned Income Tax Credit, 96
economic forces
  impacts on families, 68
Economic Policy Institute, 92, 93
Edelman, Marion Wright, 96
Edin, Kathryn, 87
education
  family disruption affects, 29, 35, 46, 55–56
  parental help with costs of, 32–33
Elshtain, Jean Bethke, 53, 71
*Embattled Paradise: The American Family in
  an Age of Uncertainty* (Skolnick), 62

English, Diane, 18
Equal Means, 88
Etzioni, Amitai, 29, 71, 72, 74

Faludi, Susan, 84, 85
families
  are seedbed of societal virtues, 31
  conflict in
    divorce generates, 37
  disruption of, 12
    conservative right views as moral
      failure, 63
    may affect generational transmission of
      wealth, 33
    social effects of, 34–36
  diversity of forms of
    public acceptance of, 22
    undermines society, 36
  egalitarianism of relationships in, 39
  impacts of economic forces on, 68
  two-parent
    media depict as source of pathology,
      18–19
    provide stable authority structure,
      37–38
  see also single-parent families
Family and Medical Leave Act, 71
family values reductionism
  scapegoats single parents, 73
fatherhood movement, 60
  challenges and goals of, 61
Forgotten Americans, The (Schwarz and
  Volgy), 92
Fortune magazine, 90
Fuchs, Victor, 21
Furstenberg, Frank, 28, 34, 41

Galston, William, 39, 40, 55, 71
Garfinkel, Irwin, 23
gender differences
  in divorce effects on children, 46–47
  in living standards after divorce, 25
  in risks from single-parent families, 29
  in stepparent relationships, 31
girls
  divorce effects on, 46–47
  risk of single-parent families to, 29
Goldman, Daniel, 55
Goode, Andrew, 67
Grandparents, Grandchildren (Kornhaber and
  Woodward), 57
Guidubaldi, John, 44, 45

Hallmark, 17, 19–20
Handlin, Oscar, 83
Hernandez, Donald, 67
Hetherington, E. Mavis, 23
Hetherington, Mavis, 47
Horn, Wade, 44

income inequality, 92
individualism, 39, 59
individual rights, 39
intergenerational poverty, 24

Jackson, Jesse, 50

John Paul II, 53
joint custody, 42
Jones, Jacqueline, 94
Judis, John, 70

Kalter, Neil, 43
Kerry, John, 82
"Kids Count Data Book" (Casey
  Foundation), 54
Kornhaber, Arthur, 57, 58
Kozol, Jonathan, 95
Krementz, Jill, 42

Lasch, Christopher, 63
Lewis, Oscar, 83
Long, Russell, 86
Los Angeles Times, 50
Luker, Kristen, 7
Lynch, David, 18

Mackey, Wade C., 49
Mandate for Change, 96
marriage
  conflict-ridden
    contributes to emotional distress in
      children, 73
    staying in for sake of children, 16
  poverty rates in, 88
  trends in, 69–70
  women have been pushed into, 99
Marriage, Divorce, Remarriage (Cherlin), 15
McDermott, John, 44, 45
McLanahan, Sara, 22, 24, 26, 32
media
  depict two-parent families as
    pathological, 18–19
  response to increase in violent crime, 50
minimum wage, 93
Mother Jones, 70
Moynihan, Daniel Patrick, 18, 82, 84
Murphy Brown, 18, 62, 71, 98
Murray, Charles, 64, 80

Nation, 98
National Center for Health Statistics, 11
National Commission on Children, 30, 32,
  56
national differences
  in divorce and out-of-wedlock births,
    38–39
National Institute for Responsible
  Fatherhood, 61
National Survey on Children, 23, 46
National Welfare Rights Organization, 86
Negro Family, The (Moynihan), 84
New England Journal of Medicine, 90
Newsweek, 64
New Yorker, 22
New York Times, 11, 55, 94
New York Times Magazine, 86
Norton, Eleanor Holmes, 60

opinion polls
  teenagers' views on divorce, 22
  on tolerance of diversity, 22
Origins, 53

out-of-wedlock births, 10
  rates of, 15, 71–72
    are linked to violent crime rates, 51
  social sanctions against, 14–15
    conservative right would restore, 63

Page, Clarence, 50, 79
parents
  aging, children's obligations to, 34
  death of, 13–14
  most require some social support, 78
  noncustodial
    lack of child contact with, 41–42
  underestimate effects of divorce on
    children, 43
People magazine, 17
Perry, Joseph, 45
Pollitt, Katha, 98
polls. *See* opinion polls
Popenoe, David, 29
popular culture
  condones divorce/unmarried parenthood,
    17–18
poverty
  culture of
    diverts attention from culture of greed,
      96
    is myth, 89
  family disintegration as cause of, 34–36,
    54
    correlation not proof of causation, 65,
      73–74
  links with unwed motherhood, 80–81
  marriage not guarantee against, 88
  rates among children, 92
    and AFDC recipients, 87
  single mothers vulnerable to, 15
Promise Keepers, 61
Putting People First (Clinton and Gore), 95

Quayle, Dan, 12, 18, 62, 71

racism
  is behind condemnation of poor women,
    76
Radical America, 90
Reed, Adolph, Jr., 90
regime effect, 39–40
Regulating the Lives of Women (Abramovitz),
  87
Regulating the Poor (Piven and Cloward), 86
research community
  and ideological pressures, 36
Rockefeller, Nelson, 30
Rosencranz, Stacey, 62

Savage Inequalities (Kozol), 95
Schroeder, Pat, 92
Schwarz, Conrad, 47
Schwarz, John, 92
*Second Chances: Men, Women, and Children
  a Decade After Divorce* (Wallerstein and
  Blakeslee), 26, 65
sexism
  is behind condemnation of poor women,
    76

sexuality
  teenage
    divorce effects on, 46–47
    risk in single-parent daughters, 29
Single Mothers and Their Children (Garfinkel
  and McLanahan), 23
single mothers/motherhood
  discrimination against, 74–75
  economic vulnerability of, 24–26
    divorced vs. never-married, 65
  family values reductionism scapegoats,
    73, 80
  is legitimate choice, 98–100
  public policy questions relating to, 77–78
single-parent families, 10
  contribute to social breakdown, 53–59
  violent crime is linked to, 49–52
  see also single mothers/motherhood
Sklar, Holly, 82
Skolnick, Arlene, 62
Skoloff, Gary, 42
Sobel, Barbara, 87
social breakdown
  single-parent families contribute to, 53–59
  unmarried mothers made scapegoats for,
    72
social sanctions
  against out-of-wedlock birth, 14–15
Social Security, 94
Solinger, Ricki, 85
Sommerville, John, 41
Spirit of Community, The (Etzioni), 29, 71
Spock, Benjamin, 85
Stack, Carol, 23
Steinem, Gloria, 21
stepparents, 21
  legal obligations of, 21
stress
  of divorce on children
    long-term effects of, 45
substance abuse
  rates higher for white women, 91

teen pregnancy
  economic factors are a root cause, 81
  inexperience of mother is problem, 75–76
This Week with David Brinkley, 50
Time magazine, 92, 94
Trilateralism (Sklar), 82

Underclass, The (Auletta), 22
unemployment
  black vs. white rates of, 93
  as cause of violent crime, 49
    media reinforce assumption, 50
    no relationship between, 51
  is linked to children's problems, 68
unemployment insurance, 93–94
Urban Institute, 93
U.S. Department of Labor, 90

values
  changes in, 19
  family, conservatives equate with nuclear
    family, 63
  neutrality of, 36

Van Derbur, Marilyn, 19
Vanity Fair, 17
Volgy, Thomas, 92

*Wake Up Little Susie: Single Pregnancy and
    Race Before* Roe v. Wade (Solinger), 85
Wallerstein, Judith, 23, 26, 28, 33, 36, 44,
    45, 65
Wall Street Journal, 64
Washington Post, 19, 44
*The Way We Never Were: American Families
    and the Nostalgia Trap* (Coontz), 19
welfare
    dependency on, 24
    need for reform of, 80
Whitehead, Barbara Dafoe, 10, 63–64, 68
White House Conference on Families,
    12
Wilson, Margo, 31
Wilson, Pete, 60, 88
Wilson, William Julius, 72

women
    African-American
        images of, 83–87
        stigmatized as "welfare queens," 85–86
    are made scapegoats for social ills, 72, 80
    changing roles of, 69–70
        as cause for social ills, 84–85
    earnings of, not equal with men's, 90
    single motherhood is legitimate choice
        for, 98–100
    substance abuse rates higher for white, 91
    were pushed into marriage in the past, 99
    work-force participation by, 21
Woodward, Kenneth L., 57, 58

Yankelovich, Daniel, 22
Young, Iris Marion, 62

Zill, Nicholas, 23, 28, 29, 34, 37, 44
Zinsmeister, Karl, 41, 64
Z magazine, 82, 83